The US Invasion of Iraq: Conspiracy and its Tragic Aftermath

Hani Fakhouri

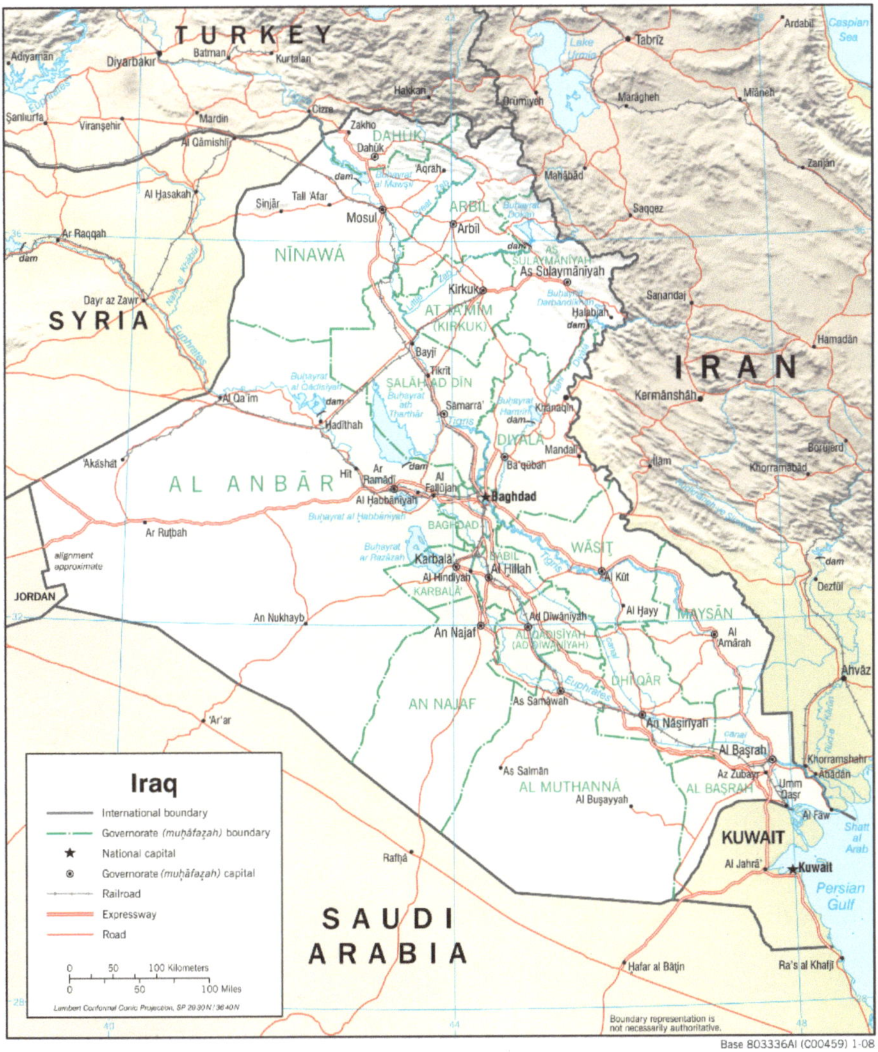

Base 803336AI (C00459) 1-08

Contents

Acknowledgements

This book is written in memory of all the innocent people who have been killed on both sides during George W. Bush's unjustified invasion of Iraq.

This study will shed light on the American invasion of Iraq in March 2003. It also reveals how ex-president George W. Bush planned the war strategy that was based on lies and fabricated secret reports to mislead the American people into supporting his aggressive policies. He continued to claim that Saddam Hussein posed a threat to U.S. security and that his weapons of mass destruction (WMD) must be destroyed to secure the safety of the American people.

It is also interesting to read how the U.S. Congress gave Bush the green light to go to war without checking to see if Iraq really posed a threat to American national security. The director of the Central Intelligence Agency (CIA), George Tenet, issued a formal report that was sent to Congress stating otherwise. He said that Iraq posed no threat to the national security of the U.S., unless American troops invaded Iraq.

In the introduction of this study, a brief historical survey will reflect that the Middle East region has been a target for foreign invasions for more than 4,000 years. The invasion of Iraq was not the first and nor will it be the last aggression by western powers against states in the Middle East.

The second chapter will reveal how Bush manipulated the mass media into supporting his invasion of Iraq. Also, analyses will reflect on the influence of lobbyists, who represent various groups that supported the American invasion. They were part of Bush's war, which they advocated to serve their own interests.

The third chapter will reflect on the active and instrumental roles of four major groups in the invasion of Iraq. The first group consists of American oil companies. Vice President Dick Cheney was closely associated with the oil companies before he was put on Bush's ticket for the White House. Cheney was part of the neoconservatives' strategy for the invasion of Iraq, which dates back to President Ronald Reagan's administration in the early 1980s. Iraq was viewed as the country with the second-largest known oil reserve in the world. Cheney publicly stated that Iraq would be the country that would sell the last barrel of oil in the world. The U.S. invasion of Iraq would open the door for American oil companies to control Iraq's oil resources after Saddam Hussein nationalized the companies in 1971.

The second group is the American neoconservative group. Most of the leadership of this group is well known to be American Jewish Zionists who are strong supporters of the state of Israel. As a matter of fact, Dr. Paul Wolfowitz, who is known as the architect of the Iraq war, is a well-known Jewish Zionist. Many members of this group have held high governmental positions, as well as positions in the American mass media.

The third group is the American Christian Evangelical Zionists, who are strong supporters of the state of Israel. They believe that the rise of the Jewish state is part of the prophecy of the coming of the Messiah.

The fourth group is the American military industrial complex. This group is very influential and played a strong role in the invasion of Iraq. It is no secret that any war the U.S. military is involved in will enhance the profitability of the companies that produce armaments, a result of more contracts with the Defense Department.

Each of these four groups has strongly supported Bush's policies in the invasion of Iraq. However, each group has its own objective and purpose behind that support.

The fourth chapter of this book focuses on the negative consequences of the war on the U.S. It was the longest war in the history of the U.S., lasting for more than eight years. More than 4,500 American soldiers died in vain and more than 32,000 soldiers were injured, many with permanent disabilities. The impact of the war created psychological problems for many of the returning veterans, which is reflected in the high suicide rate of these individuals. Furthermore, the war in Iraq created a financial burden on the American people. The cost of the war was covered by borrowing money from foreign countries, especially China.

The fifth chapter will reveal the negative consequences of the war on Iraqi society. It was reported that more than one million civilians were killed during the eight years of fighting. Also, the infrastructure was destroyed from the bombings. Even now, in 2014, there are wide shortages of electrical power and fresh water for consumption and most of the sewer systems have not been completely repaired. Furthermore, Iraq's industrial structure was destroyed, which has contributed to the high rate of unemployment. The war also led to more than four million refugees, who left to escape death. Some of the armament used by American soldiers was coated with enriched uranium, which has contaminated the physical environment in Iraq. The impact of such weapons is now reflected in the high rate of abnormal births and the increase in the rate of deaths caused by cancer. The war also revived sectarian conflicts in Iraq.

The conclusion will reflect that the war brought many negative consequences to both the U.S. and Iraq. It was a war of choice to satisfy Bush's personal ego. He is responsible for the deaths of many people and should be prosecuted a war criminal. So far, Congress has ignored the tragedy that was the war in Iraq, because they were part of the decision to implement it. Finally, the invasion of Iraq was the equivalent of putting Iraq on a silver platter and handing it to Iran. Dr. E. Alawai, the previous Iraqi prime minster, put it clearly when he stated that the only state who is the major beneficiary of the war in Iraq is Iran.

Chapter I: A Brief Historical Survey of Western Aggression in the Middle East

The history of the Middle East, especially during the past thousand years or more, reveals western aggression against the region.

The American invasion of Iraq in 2003 was a continuation of that aggression. President George W. Bush publicly referred to that invasion as a "crusaders' war."

The following question needs to be answered: Why was and is the Middle East a target to outsiders, more so than any other region around the globe?

There are several reasons behind such continuous conflicts. First, the Middle East region has served as a bridge that connects three major continents: Europe from the west, Asia from the east and Africa from the south. Throughout history, human traffic through the region was a continuous process. Some stayed and others continued their journeys to other locations around known regions.

Second, the Middle East was the birthplace of human civilization. Third, the Middle East is the birthplace of the three basic monotheistic religions: Judaism, Christianity and Islam. Conflicts among the followers of these three religions have been a problem (especially outside of the Middle East), which has influenced the political trends in the region.

Fourth, the geopolitical location of the Middle East has been a major cause of political conflicts, especially among major powers outside of the region. Those who were able to control the region were also able to protect the trade routes between the three continents. Later on, the region's strategic location was also of great importance from the perspective of a military strategy, especially during the past century.

Fifth, the Middle East region's natural resources were and still are a target to be dominated by western powers. More than two-thirds of the known oil reserves in the world are found in the region. The oil resources have been the envy of others who were eager to gain control. For such reasons and others, the region was the target of domination by foreign powers since the dawn of civilization, which was started by the ancient Greek and Roman Empires during the second and first millennium. Their occupation came to an end with the rise of Islam during the seventh century A.D. European aggression occurred again during the 10th and 11th centuries A.D. by the European Crusades.

Pope Benedictine II called on European political leaders to unite and start a crusaders' war to save Christ's land from the "infidels." The irony of such a misleading call by the highest Christian authority at the time reflects a state of ignorance and lack of awareness that the region was inhabited by the followers of the three monotheistic religions. During that period, people lived in peace with each other, irrespective of their religious affiliations. Nevertheless, the crusaders' war lasted for nearly 200 years and, at the end, they were expelled from the region.

I would like to point out that the wave of religious discrimination against Islam by Europeans began at that time. It has been increasing since then, especially since the creation of Israel in 1948 and the fall of the communist regime in the former USSR in 1989.

During the 13th century, the area was invaded by Asiatic tribes (the "Mongols"), who left a path of destruction behind. The invasion weakened the Arab Islamic Empire, which later led to the rise of the Ottoman Empire for nearly 500 years. Ottoman rule of the Arab world came to an end at the culmination of World War I in 1919 and was considered the darkest period in Arab history.

From the 19th century to the beginning of World War II, several parts of the Arab world in North Africa and part of the Arab Gulf area were under British, French, Italian and Spanish colonialist rule.

The rest of the Arab world was under the rule of the Ottoman Empire until 1919. This was known as the Fertile Crescent, which was under British and French colonialist rule. This lasted until the end of World War II.

Prior to the beginning of the war, Arabs revolted against Ottoman rule and, at the time, Britain and France promised freedom and total independence to the Arabs if they joined their forces against Ottoman rule, according to the "McMahon Paper." Under the Shareef Hussein leadership, they joined the British and French governments against the Ottomans (1914-1918). The tragedy of such an agreement was revealed later on, when both Britain and France ignored the promises they made.

According to the "Sykes-Picot" agreement between Britain and France (1919), the eastern part of the Arab world was divided into two spheres of influence by the two colonialist powers. That agreement divided the Arab world into smaller political entities, consistent with the concept of "divide and rule," which is still going on in the 21st century.

Arab political leadership at the time rejected what the British and French did. Rebellions in various parts of the Arab world against British and French colonialism ended at the culmination of World War II. However, French colonialism lasted until the early 1960s in Algeria.

The end of World War II, which led to the end of British and French colonialism, produced a new type of indirect colonialist political influence in the Arab world.

The new emerging power in the region was the U.S. In 1953, President Dwight D. Eisenhower stated publicly that the departure of the British and French colonialism from the Middle East created a political vacuum that the U.S. needed to fill. Unfortunately, U.S. foreign policy, which began to implode on the Arab world in particular and the Middle East in general, produced very negative consequences that have contributed to the political instability of the region during the past six decades. The following examples illustrate this point.

First, the creation of the state of Israel against the will of the majority of the Palestinian people in 1948 was the starting point that led to international terrorism. President Harry S. Truman admitted in his memoir that the U.S. exercised its political power at the United Nations (U.N.) to partition Palestine into an Arab state and a Jewish state in order to win the Jewish votes in New York, California and Pennsylvania during the 1948 presidential election. The creation of the Jewish state not only led to four wars (in 1948, 1956, 1967 and 1973), but also to a continuous state of hostility that still exists today (2014).

President Truman's reckless policy remains a major element of instability in the Middle East. The U.S. policy continues to provide military and financial support to a fascist state that has been suppressing the Palestinians since its creation. The creation of the state of Israel and American political and military support during the past six decades has contributed to the rise of terrorism directed mainly at the U.S., thanks to its one-sided policy. It is no longer a secret to point out that Congress is politically controlled by the American Israel Public Affairs Committee (AIPAC). It is the most influential lobby in the nation's capital. Whatever the Jewish Zionist lobby wants concerning Israel is expected to be implemented by Congress.

The irrational American foreign policy has continued in different areas of the Middle East. Examples include the various military coups the CIA has been involved in, especially for the benefit of American oil companies.

The first military coup took place in Syria in 1949. President Shukry al-Quatly, who was elected in 1946, was removed because he refused to cooperate with American oil companies. Since his removal, authoritarian military regimes replaced democratic regimes. Beginning in 1949, Syria experienced several military coups that ended with Hafiz Al-Assad taking power during the 1960s. After his death, Al-Assad's son inherited his political role, which eventually led to a civil war in March, 2011. As of 2014, the war is ongoing.

The second military coup took place in Iran in 1953, removing Dr. M. Musadag (the prime minister) from power. Dr. Musadag was democratically elected. His removal was attributed to his nationalization of the Iranian oil companies and led to the rise of Islamic militant political trends under the leadership of Ayatollah Khomeini.

The impact of American foreign policy since the end of World War II has contributed to the region's political instability.

Another act of aggression the Israeli government was part of was the 1956 Suez Canal invasion. Britain, France and Israel invaded the Suez Canal zone after Egypt nationalized it and took control of operating the passage of ships through the international waterway. The invasion turned out to be a disaster for both the British and French governments after they were ordered by the U.N. to withdraw their forces out of Egypt in 1957.

It seems at the time that the major western powers, especially Britain and France, believed they still had the right to control the destiny of the people in their previous colonies.

Another act of aggression against Egypt, Syria and Jordan was also committed by Israel in 1967. That invasion would not have taken place without the indirect support of the U.S. government.

Egypt, under the leadership of Gamal Abed il-Nasser, played an influential role in the non-aligned nations that were led by Tito of Yugoslavia and Nehru of India. The three nations did not align themselves in the Cold War, which was taking place between the U.S. and the old U.S.S.R.

John Foster Dollies, Secretary of State during the Dwight Eisenhower presidency, made things very clear in terms of American foreign policy. He said, "If you are not with us, then you are against us. There is no such thing as non-aligned nations."

Egypt, under Nasser's leadership, was not viewed positively by western powers in general and the U.S. government in particular. The idea of Arab nationalism has created an uncomfortable feeling in the west due to the future possibility of the rise of a United Arab States that would dominate what is referred to as the Arab world. For the past few hundred years, western governments have been following the strategy of "divide and rule" because it served their interests in the region.

During the past six to seven decades, western governments, and in particular the U.S., have protected the corrupt political leadership in the entire Arab world. Publicly, the U.S. always advocates democratic rule. In theory, it is true. But in practice, it is a misleading policy. The Arab world, which consists of 22 nations, did not have a single democratic government until the Arab Spring Revolution of 2010. American politicians were aware of this and continue to support the authoritarian Arab regimes against the aspirations of their people as long as they continue to implement U.S. strategy.

It is of interest to observe the reactions in western societies in general about the Arab Spring Revolution that began in Tunisia in December 2010, followed by Egypt in January 2011. American politicians in particular did not come out immediately in support of the young people's uprising. When the trends turned to favor the national revolutions, American politicians began to call on political regimes (especially in Egypt) to surrender their authority to those calling for freedom, justice and equal opportunity for all.

Despite such changes, especially on the part of President Barack Obama, some of the members of Congress have been expressing their concerns in terms of who will emerge to rule Egypt. This was reflected in the number of congressional members who have been visiting Egypt frequently to meet and talk with Egyptian political leaders. For example, Senator John McCain and Senator Lindsey Graham visited Egypt six times from 2011 to 2013.

Such political patterns of behavior on the part of American politicians are viewed by many Egyptian political activists as a direct interference in Egyptian internal political affairs. What also adds to Egyptian suspicions of American interference is when some members of Congress threaten to suspend American foreign aid to Egypt. The U.S. has been providing Egypt's military aid equal to $1.3 billion per year and another nearly $250 million in economic aid. It is also of interest to assess the Egyptian public's reactions to American foreign aid to Egypt, which was reflected in several surveys completed during 2011 and 2012. More than 75 percent of the Egyptian responses were in favor of American foreign aid being suspended. The main reason behind this is the fact that Egyptians do not want to be under the influence of the U.S. or any other foreign power. American politicians have failed to learn a lesson from the negative consequences of their foreign policies in many areas around the globe, especially the Middle East. The numerous surveys done by American organizations from 2011 to 2013 reflect a negative image of the U.S. due to its foreign policy. The average American politician is a shortsighted person. From the first day they are elected they start planning a strategy to ensure they receive financial contributions for their reelection.

This is the negative pitfall of the American political election. Despite the fact that many of those elected have the good intention of serving their constituents, they end up serving lobbyists and interest groups who provide them with most of the financial support to run again during the next election. During the past few decades, the American political election system has been plagued by the increasing cost to any politicians who run, especially for Congress or the White House. The cost of the 2012 election for both Congress and the White House was estimated to exceed $6.3 billion. Money shapes politics at both the national and international levels. As the common saying goes, "money corrupts." This is also attributed to the 2010 Supreme Court decision to lift the ceiling on political contributions to American politicians. This translates into the possibility that those with the financial resources will end up influencing the direction of the political elections in the U.S.

The U.S. Supreme Court decision is, in my judgment, in contradiction with the basic principles that the Founding Fathers set for the U.S more than 200 years ago. The U.S. dollar is in contradiction with the freedom of expression. Those who have no money cannot express their political views against those who have the means to spend millions of dollars. As the common saying reflects, "money talks."

There are more than 16,000 registered lobbyists in the nation's capital, as well as an equal number who are not registered. These organizations represent many multinational corporations, interest groups, institutions and religious and nonreligious groups who hire lobbyists to represent their interests and shape congressional bills that end up favoring them over others. What happens to the American national interest, as a whole, is a completely different matter.

During Barack Obama's 2008 presidential campaign, I had the opportunity to ask him a question during his visit to Troy, Michigan. "What will your policy be towards lobbyists if you are elected?" I asked. He responded by saying that it is a political priority of his to curtail their influence in the nation's capital.

Mr. Obama was elected as president in 2008 and was reelected in 2012 and no action has been taken to curtail the lobbyist influence. This influence continues to increase due to large monetary contributions to the election of the politicians that will serve their interests. It is of interest to note that President Obama raised more than $1 billion during his first term, which led to his re-election. Senate Majority Leader Harry Reid stated publicly in 2012 that the current Congress is the most corrupt in the history of the U.S.

The U.S. invasion of Iraq in 2003 was greatly influenced by lobbyists such as AIPAC and the neoconservatives, the oil lobby and the American military industrial complex. The main objectives of the lobbyists differ from each other, but their main goal was the invasion of Iraq. They have achieved their objective regardless of the negative consequences of the invasion of Iraq on America's national interest.

For further information on the influence of lobbyists, read "This Town" by Mark Leibovich (Penguin Group, 2013).

Chapter II: The Deceptive Strategy for the Invasion of Iraq

A decade has passed since the U.S. invasion of Iraq in 2003 and three years since the military occupation ended in 2011.

There are numerous questions that need to be raised. Was the U.S. invasion a war of choice or a necessary one? What have been the consequences of the war on both the U.S. and Iraq?

The answers to such questions are very important in shedding light on what took place behind closed doors and who was responsible for actions that led to the deaths of more than a million people. The killing of innocent people to satisfy corrupt politicians and/or to implement a political strategy set by interest groups or lobbyists representing multinational corporations—irrespective of its impact on the American national interest—is an act of treason. In such a case, those who were advocates of such a policy should be investigated and, if evidence suggests guilt, prosecuted for their crimes. In any free and truly democratic society, irresponsible elected politicians should be held accountable for their actions.

Plans for the invasion of Iraq began nearly two decades before the war by Dick Cheney (who was the Secretary of Defense in President Ronald Reagan's administration) and his undersecretary, Paul Wolfowitz. Both men were later part of George W. Bush's administration after his election in 2000.

President Bush and those surrounding him continued to plan for the invasion of Iraq and were looking for justification to implement this plan. It was made public that Bush and his corrupt team were hoping for something like a "new Pearl Harbor" to take place in order to justify the implementation their war strategy against Iraq. A year later, this negative wishful thinking was implemented by Osama bin Laden, who organized the September 11, 2001, attacks against the U.S.

After this tragedy, Bush and his team began a public campaign that placed responsibility for the attacks on Saddam Hussein. Furthermore, they promoted the idea that Iraq possessed WMD and posed a threat to the U.S. Such serious accusations were made without a shred of evidence.

The American public should know how and why the Bush administration invaded Iraq. Who prompted the invasion of Iraq and why? What have been the consequences of the war on Iraqi and American societies?

It should be noted that Saddam Hussein was not involved in the tragic September 11, 2001, attacks and that Iraq did not possess WMD. The main reasons behind the Bush administration's strategy to invade Iraq were to control Iraq's oil and remove Saddam Hussein's regime from power for Israel's benefit. Iraq was viewed as the only Arab government with the potential to threaten Israel.

At the time, the American mass media failed to investigate the administration's claims that Iraq was a threat to the U.S., as Bush and his administration stated openly. The mass media—which is greatly influenced by Israel and their supporters in the U.S.—began to dance to the beat of the music set by the White House, reinforcing the baseless claim that Iraq was a threat to the U.S. This rhetoric was set by the Bush administration even prior to the September 11 tragedy.

Ron Suskind noted in his book "The One Percent Doctrine" that, "Bush had asked Richard Clarke, the National Coordinator for Security, about Saddam's link to 9/11, Clarke said, 'definitely there is no connection found – this was clearly al-Qaeda, and al-Qaeda and Saddam were natural enemies. Furthermore, during the first National Security Council meeting in January of 2001, dealt with the overthrow of Saddam Hussein, and so did the second. It was a matter of how, not whether.[1]

George W. Bush's plan to invade Iraq began prior to the September 11 attacks against the U.S. The attacks were a gift to Bush, which he used to justify the invasion of Iraq.

Richard Clarke noted in his book, "Against All Enemies: Inside America's War on Terror" that on September 12, 2003, only al-Qaeda was guilty of the attack, but Bush was not satisfied with this answer and insisted that he and his people look again for an Iraqi connection. Clarke told him, "Absolutely, we will look – again … But you know, we have looked several times for state sponsorship of Al Qaeda and not found any real linkages to Iraq. Iran plays a little, as does Pakistan, and Saudi Arabia, Yemen." Clarke further notes that the president urged his administration to "Look into Iraq, Saddam."[2]

Clarke continued to refer to Osama Bin Laden and al-Qaeda as those responsible for the 9/11 attacks. Paul Wolfowitz, who was a member of the council and undersecretary of the Defense Department, responded to Clarke's remarks by saying "Why do you keep saying Bin Laden? It is Saddam Hussein who is responsible for the attack."

During Bush's campaign of accusing Saddam Hussein of possessing WMD, U.N. Inspector Hans Blix issued his first report that stressed no WMD were found in Iraq. Furthermore, Blix added that the supposed Iraqi threat to the U.S. was

---

[1] Suskind, Ron. *The One Percent Doctrine*. New York, New York: Simon & Schuster. 2006.

[2] Clarke, Richard. *Against All Enemies: Inside America's War on Terror*. New York, London, Toronto, Sydney: Free Press. 2004.

nothing but an act to mislead the American public and justify a U.S. invasion of Iraq.

George W. Bush made a famous statement that Iraq was an eminent threat to the security of the U.S., that Saddam Hussein's smoking gun pointed at the U.S. and that the smoke should be stopped before it turned into a mushroom cloud. This set the stage for the invasion of Iraq before the September 11 attacks.

In his book, "The Lies of George W. Bush," David Corn noted in the introduction, "George W. Bush is a liar. He has lied large and small, directly and by omission. He has mugged the truth—not merely in honest error, but deliberately, consistently and repeatedly."[3] George W. Bush, Dick Cheney and the neoconservative cabal, led by Paul Wolfowitz and Douglas Feith, began to manufacture and manipulate intelligence reports to use as evidence in their public speeches to convince the American public, as well as the American Congress, that Iraq posed a threat to the US.

False, manufactured reports by advocates of the invasion of Iraq began to circulate in the American mass media. Reports were created about such issues as the "yellow cake" uranium shipped from Niger to Iraq and the aluminum tubes that could be used for the manufacturing of WMD. In addition, there was the famous "The Mobile Biological Lab" intelligence report, which was delivered by Secretary of State Colin

Powell at the U.N. prior to the invasion. This report stressed Iraqi threats to the U.S. and Middle East region. Powell later apologized for delivering this report because it was based on false information. Despite these reports, there was not a single shred of evidence to support George W. Bush's lies to the nation about Saddam Hussein's threat to the U.S.

The Influence of the Lobbyists

Financial contribution to politicians is part of the American political campaign system and has been increasing steadily over many decades. It has enhanced political corruption and it was estimated that the money spent on the 2008 election exceeded $4.3 billion. The cost for the 2012 election increased to exceed $6 billion after the U.S. Supreme Court (in 2010) lifted the ceiling on the amount of Political Action Committee (PAC) money they can give to political candidates. Such situations tend to let the majority of the members in the U.S. Congress serve the interests of lobbyists who contribute large amounts of money to ensure the political election will serve the interest groups that these lobbyists represent. It has been reported that there are more than 16,000 registered lobbyists in the nation's capital and an equal number of lobbyists who are not

[3] Corn, David. *Lies of George W. Bush: Mastering the Politics of Deception*. New York: Three Rivers Press, 2004.

registered. In general, lobbyist political influence on national and international government policy has no regard for the American national interest.

One of the main reasons behind such political behavior on the part of many members of Congress is attributed to the fact that the majority of American voters who participate in elections are politically illiterate. In order for democracy to function properly, voters should keep track of their representatives' political activities and let them know when they disagree with their political policy. The tragedy of the political situation in the U.S. is the fact that the majority of American voters go to sleep after they cast their votes once every two or four years. For that reason and others, American politicians in general are keen on satisfying those who support them financially, as opposed to those who elected them.

I would say that money corrupted the political system, especially in 2010 when the U.S. Supreme Court decided that money is a "form of speech." In my judgment, this is in contradiction with the meaning of equality in a democratic society. Those who have the financial resources tend to have more political rights and privileges than those who are deprived of such financial resources. The concept of "equal rights" is meaningless in this type of American democracy.

James Bennet, in an article titled "New Price of American Politics," published in the Atlantic Journal in September 2012, presents an interesting historical survey of financial contributions to political candidates. He concludes his analysis by stating, "This is a legalized-bribery kind of system, where no one has to say anything. I don't have to say what I want—you know what I want."[4] The American Congress has turned into a powerful agency to work for the benefit of the rich and powerful at the expense of their constituents, who voted them into that institution.

In their article "Money in Politics," Bill Moyers and Bernard Weisberger asked where the outrage was, stating, "… once again, distract the public's attention from the death rattle of American democracy brought on by an overdose of campaign cash."[5] They continued to say that a radical minority of the super-rich has gained ascendency over politics, buying the policies, laws, tax breaks, subsidies and rules that consolidate a permanent state of vast inequality by which they can further help themselves to America's wealth and resources. They write, "… what's happening to the U.S. political system is corruption—a deep, systematic corruption."

It is so obvious and clear that lobbyists in the nation's capital play an influential role in shaping American foreign and national policy in favor of those whom they

---

[4] Bennett, James. "The New Price of American Politics." The Atlantic. 19 Sept. 2012.

[5] Moyers, Bill. Weisberger, Bernard. "Money in Politics." Moyers & Company. 20. Aug. 2012

represent. The four major groups who advocated the Iraq invasion through their lobbyists by influencing members of Congress include:

- The neoconservatives and AIPAC
- The American oil companies
- The American military industrial complex
- The American evangelical Christian and Jewish Zionist groups

All of these groups had a common objective: the invasion of Iraq and the removal of Saddam Hussein from power. However, each one of these groups has their own agenda, which will be discussed later. The forthcoming analysis will reflect that their efforts toward and support of the Iraq invasion was not consistent with American national interest in the Middle East region.

George Tenet, CIA director during the Bush administration, declassified a letter that was sent on October 18, 2002, to Senator Bob Graham, Chairman of the Senate Committee. The letter, which was read at a joint hearing of the House and Senate Intelligence Committee, reflected the fact that Saddam Hussein was not an imminent threat to the security of the U.S. and that he would not use any of his chemical and biological weapons against the U.S. unless attacked first. The letter reiterated, "… that is, he would only use these weapons in self-defense."

The letter clearly reflects that Saddam Hussein would not use any of his weapons except in self-defense, which meant if the U.S. attacked him first, only then would he retaliate. The declassified CIA letter could have been read by any member in the U.S. Congress. The irony is that no information exists that can be referred to in terms of how many members of Congress have read the letter. My guess is not too many, for the simple fact that the majority of the members of Congress were inclined to support the invasion despite the letter's existence. On October 11, 2002, in a joint session, the majority of the members gave George W. Bush the authority to go to war.

All of the Republicans and 81 Democrats in the House supported the war resolution. In the Senate, only one Republican voted against the resolution. In addition, 29 Democrats supported the resolution and 21 voted against it. The passage of the war resolution did not come as a surprise, despite the CIA declassified letter, which stated that Iraq did not pose any threat to the U.S.

The American political system is corrupt. As a matter of fact, the influence of pressure groups and lobbyists on the members of the American congress is no longer a hidden fact.

Mark Leibovich stated in his book "This Town" that lobbyists spend as much as $3.5 billion per term on politicians, in order to implement the strategy of those they represent. Furthermore, he stated that what they contribute to politicians is an insignificant amount compared to what they are getting in return from the government's $3.5 trillion budget.

The influence of money on the conduct of politicians has led to their moral and political corruption. As a matter of fact, Harry Reid, the Senate Majority Leader, stated publicly in 2012 that Congress is the most corrupt in the history of the U.S. Mr. Leibovich's book[6] referred to the impact of political-influence peddling, which has led to major political corruption. He further referred to a quote published by Ramsay MacMillan, a distinguished Yale historian who has written extensively on ancient Rome. MacMillan published a book that took on one of the central questions in his field: Why did the greatest empire in the history of the world collapse in the fifth century? The root-cause, he explained, was the political corruption that had become systemic in the late Roman Empire.

Nevertheless, some advocates of war were calling for the invasion of Iraq before the war resolution was even introduced. A well-known member of the House, Democrat Jim Moran, was invited by a women's church group in Virginia to explain why Congress supported the invasion of Iraq. During his presentation, he said, among other things, that Jewish groups were calling for the invasion of Iraq. His speech was highlighted by the mass media the following day and he was pressured to apologize publicly for his remarks.

Scott McClellan, former White House press secretary in the Bush administration, noted in his book, "What Happened: Inside the Bush White House and Washington's Culture of Deception" that the American people were convinced of the validity of the Iraq war through Bush's "…sophisticated political propaganda campaign," the purpose of which was to manipulate "sources of public opinion" and downplay "the major reasons for going to war."[7]

He also described Vice President Dick Cheney as "the magic man" who "steered policy behind the scenes while leaving no fingerprints." Various groups, lobbyists, multi-national corporations and foreign governments were behind the scene pushing for the invasion of Iraq and the removal of Saddam Hussein from power. All have a common target, but each group has their own individual agenda to achieve.

---

[6] Leibovich, Mark. *This Town*. New York: The Penguin Group, 2013.

[7] McClellan, Scott. *What Happened: Inside the Bush White House and Washington's Culture of Deception*. United States: PublicAffairs, 2009.

Chapter III: The Advocates of the Invasion in Iraq

The advocates of the U.S. invasion of Iraq are the American oil companies, the neoconservatives, the Christian evangelicals and the military industrial complex.

The American Oil Companies and their Lobbyists

Since World War II, the Middle East has experienced a wave of nationalistic upheaval directed against western colonialism in the region. The tides of nationalistic movements led, among other things, to a new trend of nationalization of foreign oil companies in the region. In 1953, the CIA and the British secret service plotted to overthrow Iran's newly elected Prime Minister, Dr. Mohammad Mossadegh, and restore the shah back to his throne. The major reason behind the plot is attributed to the Prime Minister Mossadegh nationalization of Iran's oil, "the BP."

This foreign colonialist act, especially on the part of the U.S. government, was meant to send a message to political leaders in the oil-producing countries to discourage them from entertaining a similar adventure like the Iranian one. President Eisenhower publicly acknowledged the CIA venture and stated that the departure of the British and the French from the Middle East region created a vacuum that the U.S. needed to fill. What this really meant to the population in the region was that the new colonialist power would be the U.S. government.

The blunder that the U.S. government committed against Iran during the early 1950s led to the revolution of Ayatollah Khomeini, which could be seen in our days as a challenge to the U.S. foreign policy in the region.

The removal of political leaders from their positions—even if they were freely elected by their own people—predates the Eisenhower presidency. In 1946, Syria freely elected President Shukri al-Quwatli, who opposed the Trans-Arabian pipeline "Tapline," which would take oil from Iraq through Syria to the Lebanese Mediterranean port of Sidon. Quwatli was replaced by a dictator Military General Husni al-Zaim[8]. This military coup led to several others, until Hafiz Al-Assad took over in the 1960s.

Despite the U.S.' direct threats and its covert activities in the Middle East region, all Arab oil-producing governments nationalized their foreign oil companies. The

---

[8] Douglas Little, "Cold War and Covert Action: the United States and Syria, 1945-1958." Middle East Journal, 44 America. Jan. 1, 1990.

political act started by the Iraqi government nationalized its foreign oil company in 1972. The U.S. government responded with an oil embargo against Iraq, but it didn't last long and was lifted in 1975. The American oil companies and their political supporters did not allow the Iraqi government's act of nationalizing oil companies to be forgotten.

Dick Cheney, who was Secretary of Defense during Reagan's tenure as President, began to plot the invasion of Iraq with the help of members of the new conservative group under the leadership of Paul Wolfowitz, who is referred to as the architect of the Iraq war.

After the election of George Bush Sr. in 1988, the neoconservatives began to pressure the Bush administration to invade Iraq. The plotting was partially successful and led to the 1991 Gulf War, but American troops didn't invade Iraq. Another attempt by the neoconservatives was to pressure President Clinton to invade Iraq. He dismissed the pressure, but heavily bombed Iraq under phony pretext.

After the election of George W. Bush as president and Dick Cheney as vice president, the plotting of the invasion of Iraq began to take place.

Aware of the lucrative financial return behind the invasion of Iraq, the major rationale behind the invasion—at least on the part of Bush and Cheney—was to control the Iraqi oil.

Cheney publicly acknowledged the huge oil reserve in Iraq and said that Iraq will be the country that sells the last barrel of oil. Iraq in particular is considered at the present to be classified as second to Saudi Arabia in terms of its known oil reserve, which has been estimated at 112 billion barrels. Furthermore, geological reports reveal that Iraq is sitting on a pool of oil that might exceed 300 billion barrels. That makes Iraq not only a target to acquire by the U.S., but many other international oil companies.

According to the Financial Times (March 20, 2008), the so-called "Oil and Energy" working group of the U.S. State Department, which met four times in 2002 and 2003 and included influential Iraqi exiles, had put forward the idea as a crucial plank in Iraq's postwar reconstruction plans, increased foreign participation in Iraq's postwar reconstruction plans, increased foreign participation in Iraqi's oil industry, members argued, would help revitalize its most important economic lifeline ravaged by years of neglected and underinvestment under Saddam's regime. But it would get U.S. oil companies close to Iraq's reserves, which remain significantly under-exploited compared to those of other big producers and which, according to some geologists, could hold the world's largest deposits, surpassing even those of Saudi Arabia.

The article continues to note, "Dick Cheney called for greater access in 1999 came into place, the U.S.-backed Ahmad Chalabi, a man who famously said in

2002 that 'U.S. oil companies will have a big shot at Iraqi oil' - to chair Iraq's Energy Council." Ahmad Chalabi, who was living in exile for few decades and was well known as a thief, a liar and an embezzler, and who is wanted to serve a jail sentence in Jordan for bank theft, turned out to be a consultant and an adviser to the U.S. government and oil companies.

This makes any person who is familiar with Chalabi's background wonder about American policymakers who were involved with and relied on such characters for policy formation. Those policymakers were helping to reverse the Iraqi oil nationalization of 1972. Nevertheless, there are other groups beside the American oil companies who were pushing for the invasion of Iraq, also with "oil benefit" in mind for Israel.[9]

Many neoconservatives are well known not only as Jewish Zionists, but also as extreme supporters of Israel, and were assured by Ahmad Chalabi that Iraqi oil would flow into Israel after the invasion of Iraq. On June 20, 2003, Israeli Prime Minister Benjamin Netanyahu stated during a meeting with investors in Israel, "Soon, we will see Iraq oil flowing through the old Iraqi 'IPC' lines from Karkouk to Haifa." This promise, made by Ahmad Chalabi, has not yet materialized.[10]

In her article "What Congress Really Approved: Benchmark No. 1: Privatizing Iraq's Oil for US Companies" Ann Wright noted, "On Thursday, May 24, the US Congress voted to continue the war in Iraq. The members called it 'supporting the troops.' I call it stealing Iraq's oil - the second-largest reserves in the world." Since the invasion of Iraq, the Bush administration has been working hard to privatize Iraqi oil. To add pressure on the Iraqi government, the American Congress threatened to hold U.S. construction funds that were promised to the Iraqis to rebuild what the U.S. had destroyed there.

Wright continued, "The privatization law, written by American oil company consultants hired by the Bush administration, would leave control with the Iraq National Oil Company for only 17 of the 80 known oil fields. The remainder (two-thirds) of known oil fields, and all yet undiscovered ones, would be up for grabs by the private oil companies of the world … The $120 billion dollar 'Support the Troops' legislation passed by Congress requires Iraq, in order to get reconstruction funds from the United States, to privatize its oil resources and put them up for long term (20- to 30-year) contracts."[11] This is nothing but an act of

---

[9] www.aljazeera.net (12/6/2007)

[10] Bakir, Ali. H. "Iraqi Oil and Israel." www.aljazeera.net. December 16, 2007.

new American colonization, keeping troops in Iraq to protect American oil companies' interests.

During the last two years of the Bush's administration, the U.S.'s real intention behind the invasion of Iraq was clear: the control of Iraqi oil. The U.S. government drafted a law regarding the privatization of Iraqi oil, and began to apply pressure on the Maliki government to implement it. He was asked to reconvene the Iraqi parliament to implement the proposed law before the end of George W. Bush's presidency (2008). However, the Iraqi government stalled and put the U.S. proposal on the backburner.

The U.S.-proposed law given to the Iraqi government called for the following: permitting Al-Muhafazat governments such as Kurdistan and al-Basra to sign oil contracts with foreign oil companies for a long period (25-35 years) for the production and sale of oil. The revenue from oil sale to be shared with the central government in Baghdad where there is no oil production.

This area is also dominated by Sunni Muslims, while the other two regions where oil is located are dominated by Kurds in the North and Shiites in the South. The proposal indirectly calls for the partitioning of Iraq into three regions: Kurdish in the North, Sunni in the Center, and Shiites in the South. This idea was even proposed during the Bush administration by Senator Joe Biden, who is currently vice president in the Obama administration.

History is repeating itself: conquer, divide and rule. As a matter of fact, the Kurdish government has already signed oil contracts with foreign oil companies, but the Iraqi central government rejected such agreements.

Nevertheless, the U.S. oil proposal is still being ignored by the Iraqi government and was not sent to parliament for discussion as of 2009. I doubt that very much, that even after the upcoming election of new parliament in Iraq, that the Bush's oil proposal even will be considered.

The question that ought to be explored is: what led to the invasion of Iraq? It is clear and beyond any doubt that the answer is the control of Iraqi oil. Alan Greenspan, the previous chairman of the U.S. Federal Reserve Bank, stated in his recent book, "The Age of Turbulence: Adventures in a New World" that "the invasion of Iraq, was to control Iraqi oil and domination of the Middle East as a dominant power of the region."[12]

---

[11] Ann Wright, "Privatizing Iraqi Oil", The Wisdom Fund, www.twf.org, May 7, 2008.

[12] Greenspan, Alan. "The Age of Turbulence in a New World." New York: Pengruin PHC. 2007.

American oil companies, as well as many members of Congress, were aware of the fact that American oil production at home is on a steady decline, while the need for fossil energy is increasing at a rapid rate. The U.S. is the largest consumer of fossil

energy in the world. Its population constitutes around 6% of the world population and consumes nearly one-third of oil consumption worldwide. The U.S. imports around 58% of its daily consumption from other oil-producing nations. Until recently (2008) the US imported the equivalent of 20-21 million barrels of oil daily. More than 50% of the imported oil comes from the western hemisphere such as Canada, Mexico, and Venezuela. Also, the U.S. consumption during the next 20 years has been estimated to increase by 30% (2007-2008).

U.S. oil consumption has been increasing gradually, and its oil production in the U.S. has steadily been decreasing. Until recently, U.S. local production reached its peak of 6.2 million barrels per day and will drop to nearly 4.7 million barrels per day by the year 2025, according to the U.S. Energy Information projection of future U.S. consumption.*

In addition, to the continuous pressing needs for more fossil fuels for U.S. consumption, global situation and the increasing demands for oil impacted American foreign policy. The emergence of China and India in particular on the global economic stage reflecting a rapid increase and demand for more oil created a feeling of uneasiness for the U.S. This situation played a role in influencing the U.S. invasion of Iraq for the following reasons:

- Earlier, a reference was made that Iraq has the potential of becoming the largest oil producer in the world, even passing Saudi Arabia, which—as of 2013—ranked number one. Iraq's known oil reserve exceeds 112 billion barrels in addition to its potential, which has been estimated by geologists to exceed 300 billion barrels.

*This situation began to change during 2013, when oil companies began producing oil from black rocks. This will enable the U.S. to become self-sufficient during the following few years.

- Another important economic advantage is the economic cost to produce the oil at

a cheaper rate; between $1.00 - $2.00 per barrel, compared to $25 - $30 per barrel.

- Controlling Iraq will put American oil companies in an advantageous position in securing concession to prospect, produce, and market Iraqi oil.

- Controlling Iraqi oil will provide the U.S. government the influence to meet challenges from other Arab oil-producing countries in the Gulf area in terms of oil production that influence oil prices.

- Controlling Iraqi oil will discourage other oil-producing countries from demanding to be paid in other currencies instead of U.S. dollars as Iran and Kuwait have done recently (2007-2008).

- Controlling Iraqi oil will minimize the possibility of any future attempt by other Arab oil-producing countries from using their oil as a political weapon, similar to what happened during the early 1970s Arab oil embargo, which was initiated by Saudi Arabia.

- Controlling Iraqi oil will influence where the money from the sale of oil will be invested.

These are among the most important rationale that the Bush administration calculated as a future reward for American oil companies and the U.S. government. I doubt very much that such a vision will materialize.

The Neo-Conservative Group

The Neo-Conservative group played a very effective role as an advocate of the invasion of Iraq, which occurred under false pretenses. Among the most active of the individuals in this cabal is Dr. Paul Wolfowitz, who is known to be the architect of the Iraq War. He served as Deputy Secretary of Defense, and as of former President Bush's National security advisors. Bush later appointed him as the head of the World Bank. Shortly after his appointment, he was pressured to resign from his position due to unethical conduct.

Another active member of the Neo-Con cabal and an associate of Dr. Wolfowitz is Douglas Feith, who served as undersecretary of defense for policy and policy advisor of the Pentagon. An extreme Jewish Zionist and supporter of Israel, he manipulated intelligence reports to support the invasion of Iraq. A report prepared by the Department of Defense's inspector general for Carl Levin, the Democratic Chairman of the Armed Services Committee, clearly shows how "former Under Secretary of Defense for Policy, Douglas Feith, used his Department of Defense position to cook intelligence claiming a connection between the terrorist organization and Saddam Hussein's regime..." (Truth Out Issues, April 6, 2007).

Dr. Feith is not an exception in comparison to other members of the Neo-Con cabal. Mr. J. Lewis "Scooter" Libby, who served as former Vice President Dick Cheney's Chief of Staff and as an advisor on the Middle East, is serving a jail sentence for perjury (2005). Another member of the Neo-Con cabal is David

Wurmser who also served as an advisor for Cheney on Middle Eastern affairs, according to Newsweek (March/22/2004).

He was assigned to pose through raw intelligence reports especially to see if there is a possible link between Saddam Hussein and al-Qaeda. He is also a Zionist and extreme supporter of Israel. Craig Unger in his article "They Wanted the Lies They Needed", published in Vanity Fair in July 2006, noted that "it is possible that from its very inception in the Niger operation (yellow cake) was aimed at starting an invasion in Iraq."

As early as 1992, Neo-Conservative hawks in the administration of George Bush under the aegis of Secretary of Defense Donald Rumsfeld and Vice President Dick Cheney, unsuccessfully lobbied for regime change in Iraq as part of a grandiose vision for American supremacy in the next century." Mr. Unger continued to note that "During the Clinton era, the Neo-Cons persisted with their policy goals, and they twice lobbied President Clinton to bring down Saddam Hussein. The second attempt came in the form of 'an open letter to the president' by leading Neo-Cons, many of whom later played key roles in the Bush administration, where they became known as Vulcans. Among those who signed were Michael Ledeen, John Bolton, Douglas Feith, Richard Perle, Donald Rumsfeld, David Wurmser, and others."

President Clinton's response at the time was to use some excuses to heavily bombard Iraq but not invade it. Mr. Unger continued to note that the "forged record of the phony uranium deal between Niger and Iraq where Michael Ledeen possibly has played a role in it to start the war in Iraq."

President Bush used the phony intelligence report "the yellow cake" in his State of the Union address (January 2003) referring to the "smoking gun over the U.S. that he does not want to see turning into a mushroom cloud." The Neo-Cons' main objective was the removal of "Saddam Hussein's regime and the elimination of his Ba'ath political party," which calls for the creation of Arab unity. In theory, this idea of Arab unity would create more concern in Israel and the Western world as well. As long as the Arab world is divided, it is easy to manipulate and control.

In the article "Rapture and Rupture," New York Times columnist Maureen Dowd pointed out that, "Influential Jewish conservatives inside and outside the administration, have been fierce in supporting a war on Saddam, thinking it could help Israel by scrambling the Middle East map and encouraging democracy." Dowd's suggestion that Jews in the Bush administration were putting Israel's interests over those of the U.S.

The Iraq war was about Israel, Bush insiders suggest, by E. McKay – "Yahoo of one World (3/30/04). IPS", uncovered the remarks by Phillip Zelekow, who was the executive director of the body set to investigate the terrorist attacks on the United States in September 2001. The 9/11 commission in which he suggests a prime motive for the invasion in 2003 was to eliminate a threat to Israel, a staunch U.S. ally in the Middle East. Mr. Zelekow repeated the same rationale at the University of Virginia on September 10, 2002, speaking on a panel on foreign policy experts assessing the impact of 9/11 and the future of the war on al-Qaeda. He pointed out, "Why would Iraq attack America or use nuclear weapons against us? I'll tell you what I think the real threat is and actually has been since 1990 – it's the threat against Israel!"

In his university speech, Mr. Zelekow who strongly backed attacking the Iraqi dictator, also explained the threat to Israel by arguing that Baghdad was preparing in 1990-1991 to spend huge amounts of "scarce hard currency" to harness communications against "electromagnetic pulse," a side effect of a nuclear explosion that could sever radio, electronic, and electrical communication. Mr. Zelekow served on the President's Foreign Intelligence Board (PFIAB).

The George W. Bush administration appointed many Neo-Cons, Zionist extremists in high federal government offices who were staunch supporters of Israel. They have successfully changed the Bush strategy. Instead of fighting Bin-Laden and his al-Qaeda, they shifted the war toward Saddam Hussein.

After the tragic attack of 9/11, the Neo-Cons hoped for something like Pearl Harbor to give them national justification to invade Iraq. The Bin-Laden (9/11) attack fulfilled the Neo-Cons wishes. The irony of such conduct has been ignored by the mass media, politicians and the public. Normal people who love their country will wish it well and not ill or evil. Wishing for a tragic event to happen in one's own country reflects nothing but an "un-American" attitude.

The Neo-Cons conducted a massive campaign in support of the invasion of Iraq in order to implement their agenda, which is the "removal of Saddam Hussein regime." This campaign continued despite the fact that George Tenant, the CIA director, stated that Iraq poses no threat to the U.S. In addition, Bin Laden was the one responsible for the 9/11 attacks. Despite all the evidence that pointed to Bin-Laden, the Bush administration in its entirety advised the president to invade Iraq, instead of Afghanistan, and remove Saddam Hussein from power.

The Neo-Conservative Jewish Zionist extremists played a critical role in advocating the U.S. invasion for the benefit of Israel. Political thinkers such as Francis Fukuyama called for critical evaluation of Neo-Conservative influence on U.S. foreign policy (New York Times, (May 27, 2006). The Neo-Cons and their supporters played different scenarios. The initial stage was supporting the Iraqi invasion, and the second stage was denying the responsibility for the invasion.

The Neo-Cons, led by Paul Woflowitz and some of their affiliated journals such as the Weekly Standard led by W. Kristol who was the leading promoter of the Iraqi invasion, developed a new political strategy to blame others for the Iraq war blunder. Their new strategy was that the invasion was right, but the people responsible for the war were wrong. Richard Perle noted in Vanity Fair that he regrets the situation in Iraq and if he had to re-asses his thoughts, he would have thought of a different strategy. He continued to say that those policy makers in the Bush administration should be accountable, including Bush himself.[13]

This shift became obvious to some analysts and politicians, but not too many came out publicly to point their finger at the real rationale behind the invasion of Iraq. This awareness created an uncomfortable feeling among prominent Neo-Conservatives, especially the extreme Zionists such as R. Perle, D. Feith, and others. In an article titled "Now They Tell Us," David Rose wrote in Vanity Fair (November 3, 2006), "As Iraq slips further into chaos, the war's Neo-Conservatives boosters have turned sharply on the Bush administration, charging that their grand designs have been undermined by White House incompetence … Richard Perle, Kenneth Adelman, David Frum, and others play the blame game with shocking frankness. Target No. 1: the president himself."

The blame for the failure of the Iraq war also extended to high-ranking Israeli officials. In a recent book, "Sixty Years of Israeli Secret Service: Look from the Inside," written by two retired secret service generals, Amos Gelow and Ifraeem Labeed and published by the Israeli secret service (in Hebrew), both generals expressed regrets about the exaggeration of Saddam Hussein's WMD. It is no longer a secret that the Israeli Secret Service played an active role in encouraging the Bush administration to invade Iraq in 2003.

In an article that appeared in the Charleston Daily Post Courier on May 6, 2004, former Senator Fritz Holling, Democrat of South Carolina, asked the question, "With Iraq no threat, why invade a sovereign country?" He also wrote, "The answer: President Bush's policy to secure Israel. Led by Paul Wolfowitz, Richard Perle, and Charles Krauthammer, for years there had been domino school of thought that the way to guarantee Israel's security is to spread democracy in the area [sic]." He continued to say "Bush's failed Middle East policy is creating more terrorism." Hollings cited the role of the American Israel Public Affairs Committee (AIPAC), the most important pro-Israel lobby group in Washington, in determining U.S. policy in the Middle East. "You can't have an Israel policy other than what AIPAC gives you around here. I have followed them mostly in the main, but I have also resisted signing certain letters from time to time to give the poor president a chance." Furthermore, he stated, "No president takes office – I don't care whether it is Republican or a Democrat – that all of a sudden AIPAC will tell him exactly what the policy is and senators and members of

---

[13] Aljazeera. November 4, 2006.

Congress out to sign the letters [sic]." Senator Hollings was willing to defy the pro-Israel lobby, because he was serving his final term in Washington. Senator Hollings continued to express his views regarding the abuse of "AIPAC" of their influence on the American Congress. In an article provided by "Truth Out," June 23, 2004, states, "The United States has lost its moral authority." He wrote that in 1996, a task force was formed in Jerusalem including Richard Perle, Douglas Feith, and David Wurmser. They submitted a plan for Israel to incoming Prime Minister Benjamin Netanyahu, called 'Clean Break'. It proposed that negotiations with the Palestinians be cut off and instead, the Middle East be made friendly to Israel by democratizing itself. First, Lebanon would be bombed, then Syria invaded, on the pretext of WMD. The plan was rejected by Netanyahu. Later, with the election of George W. Bush, Perle took on the Defense Policy Board. Rumsfeld, Wolfowitz, and Feith became one, two, and three of the defense department and Cheney as Vice President, took "Scooter" Libby and David Wurmser as his deputies. 'Clean Break' was streamlined to go directly into Iraq."

It is very interesting that the Neo-Cons tried to justify their policy of aggression under the false pretense that the objective of their campaign is to "spread democracy in the Middle East." The irony of this hypocrisy is the fact that they have never criticized Israel for its discrimination against Israeli Christians and Muslims, who are living in Israel. While Israeli human rights organization on numerous occasions criticized Israel for its treatment of Palestinians within the green line of the Jewish state, the situation in the occupied West Bank of Gaza, and the treatment of the Palestinians by the Israeli military establishment is nothing but a tragedy.

Those who keep talking about the Holocaust and have experienced extreme pain and death at the hands of the fascist regime in Germany should be more sensitive to the agony of the Palestinians. To put it mildly, "the victims turned out to be the victimizers." Nevertheless, the Neo-Cons have succeeded in removing Saddam Hussein's government and the ideology of the Ba'ath political party from power. The Neo-Cons have also implemented their intended agenda by putting Iraq fifty years behind. The progress that has been accomplished in Iraq during the past four to five decades has been demolished beyond expectation. The most serious damage that has been done to the Iraqi society is the disintegration of its professional class, who were the backbone of its progress.

The Christian Evangelical Zionist Groups

The third group that also played an active political role in support of the Iraqi invasion is the Christian Zionists. This group's support is based on their version of Biblical interpretation, that the rise of the state of Israel signifies the coming of the Messiah, which according to them will lead to converting many Jews into Christians.

The New York Times noted on November 14, 2006, that "For Evangelical Supporting Israel is God's Foreign Policy.[sic]" D. Kirkpatrick pointed out that the alliance of Israel, its evangelical Christian supporters and President Bush has never been closer or more potent. He continued to say that, "White evangelicals make up about a quarter of the electorate. Whatever strains may be creeping into the Israeli-American alliance over Iraq, the Palestinians and Iran, a large part of the Republican Party's base remains committed to a fiercely pro-Israel agenda that seems likely to have an effect on policy choices."

The Israeli government and its American allies have been building their alliance with evangelicals for decades. Israeli officials began working closely with John Hagee and his church, for example a quarter century ago, when he met several times with Menachem Begin (prime minister of Israel) at that time. Mr. Hagee published several books focusing on the interpretation of the religious prophecies regarding the second coming of the Messiah. Among the hardcore evangelical leaders with strong support for Israel is Dr. James Dobson, founder of "Focus on the Family." Gary Bauer also leads a major evangelical church in San Antonio and influential fundraiser for Israel.

Another evangelical leader is Marvin Olasky, is the editor of the magazine, *World*, and a Bush advisor, is a strong supporter of Israel. Pat Robertson, the producer of the 700 Club, a Virginia-based Christian broadcasting network, is also a strong advocate of Israel and anti-Islam. According to the BBC, in his broadcast, he said, "Islam is not a religion of peace, and the goal of Islam, ladies and gentlemen whether you like it or not, is world domination." He further said that Islamists were inspired by demonic power.

Mr. Robertson, who says his program is watched by millions of Americans daily, has come under intense criticism for suggesting that Americans agents should assassinate Venezuelan President Hugo Chavez. (BBC News March 14, 2008).

Many of these evangelical preachers are using religion for personal gain and influence; they especially thrive on the poor and the less educated public. When they call or support killing regardless the reasons, this is not Christianity. The God that is in the Bible, Torah and Koran preached love, compassion and justice, not violence.

Evangelical political leaders such as George Bush and the ex-candidate for the Republican Party, Sarah Palin, Governor of Alaska, told ministry students at her former church that the U.S. sent troops to fight in the Iraq war are on a "task that is from God." (Washington Post.com September 4, 2009). These types of politicians hide behind religion to justify killing innocent people for political gain.

Vincent Bugliosi pointed out that, "As has been reported often, Bush said he was called by God" to seek the presidency, and said, "I believe that God wants me to be president," and who he was, whether to go to war in Iraq he responded, "You know, he is the wrong father to appeal to in terms of strength. There is a higher father, I appeal to."

The Christian Zionists have been influenced by the Oxford Bible version that has been edited by Mr. C.I Scofield at the turn of the 20th Century (1907-1908). Mr. Scofield cooperated secretly with Jewish Zionist individuals in New York to insert short sentences and footnotes in the Bible that will support the creation of the future Jewish state. Mr. Scofield's reputation at that time was negative. He was known as a felon and an overall dishonest man who lived the high life.[14]

Military-Industrial Complex

The fourth influential group and their lobbyists who advocated the invasion of Iraq directly and indirectly is the military-industrial complex. Richard Perle, who led the Pentagon National Security advisory board, many of whose members were high-ranking official of companies that produces armaments, were advocates of the invasion of Iraq. A few weeks before the invasion, *The Wall Street Journal* referred to that group's support of the war, because they "smell profit in the air of war."

The American military industrial complex is a very powerful group that plays an influential role with members of Congress. Since the end of World War II, their influence has been steadily increasing as a result of the Cold War. Armament

---

[14] Bugliosi, Vincent. *The Prosecution of George W. Bush for Murder*. Vanguard Press, 2008.

*For further information on the new edition of the Bible by Oxford University Press and MR. J.S. Scofield editing role see the following:

a) Joseph M. Canfield. The Incredible Scofield and his Book. Ross House Books; 2nd edition, Oct. 20, 2005.

b) C.E. Carlson, The Source of the Problem in the Mid East – Part II: Why Judeo-Christians Support War

c) Listen to "Kulture II. How Oxford University Press and C.I Scofield Stole the Christian Bible" on WHTT Internet Talk Radio. Also available on tape.

production and modern weapon systems were easily justified due to the "Communist threat," which was used as a justification for more defense spending. The more money allocated for armament production, the higher their margin of profit.

There is always a profit to be made from war. It will not be the American soldiers for sure, but it will be those who are running the military productions of the military industrial complex. Over the years, the leaders of the complex have succeeded through their lobbyists in pressuring members of Congress in support of increases of the defense budget. The term used by the representatives of the military industrial complex against those members in Congress who oppose more money for defense, is "soft on national security."

Such labels reflect negatively on those members of Congress who oppose military budget increase. For that reason and others, the military industrial complex in most cases end up getting what they pushed for with the help of the Pentagon. This is reflected in the defense budget. The U.S. government spent more on defense than all members of NATO, in addition to China and Russia.

President Eisenhower's "military-industrial complex" speech warned of the abuse of the American military defense establishment and its unrealistic programs. He noted in his farewell speech to the nation that, "We have been compelled to create a permanent armaments industry of vast proportions, added to this three and a half million men and women are directly engaged in the defense establishment. We annually spend on military security more than the net income of all United States corporations," he continued to say that: "This conjunction of an immense military establishment and a large arms industry is now in the American experience. The total influence – economic, political, and even spiritual – is felt in every city, every state house, and every office of the federal government." In his speech, he emphasized that, "In the councils of government, we must guard against the acquisition of unwarranted influence, whether sought or unsought by the military industrial complex. The potential for the disastrous rise of misplaced power exists and will persist."[15]

Furthermore, he warned the American people to be aware and not to elect a president who is not aware of how the Pentagon operates. His prophecy turned out to be true. The American people elected Ronald Reagan in 1980. At that time, the U.S. was the biggest creditor nation in the world and its total debt was less than one trillion dollars. By the end of the 1988, the U.S. became the biggest debtor nation in the world, with the estimated amount of borrowed money exceeding $3.5 trillion. This money was spent on armaments.

---

[15] Military Industrial Complex – 1doc (42-KB)

More than fifty years have passed and President Eisenhower's words are still true today. The impact of the military industrial complex is more influential and fearful. The annual U.S. Defense budget reflects the influence of the Military Industrial on Congressional members.

A. Robert noted in his article, "The War We Deserve" Foreign policy, (November – December, 2007), that the U.S. Defense expenditures have grown substantially during the Bush administration by roughly 40% in inflation adjusted terms from 2000-2006."

The military industrial complex thrives on global unrest and conflicts, which are used as a justification for more spending on military production under the banner of the "American National Security." This sector of the American economy is one of the most profitable business sectors in the U.S. The armament industries especially in France, Britain, Germany, Russia, Israel, China, and Brazil are not an exception to the rule.

Bush and his administration had militarized foreign policy with the help of Bin Laden, who is the main reason for the emergence of the new concept, 'terrorism" which has been used to replace communism as the demon in western societies. Bush used the terrorism concept as a threat to American security and national interest. The fear of terrorism which has been used by the Bush administration and continuously repeated in the mass media led to the creation of a state of panic in the mind of the average American and gave President Bush political advantages which led to the abuse of executive privileges, all under the pretext of the threat of "terrorism."

In fact, terrorism under his presidency increased by more than 300%. Various sectors within the Military Industrial Complex have done their own share of creating fears about the security of the U.S. as reflected in the following: major military space industries are using massive public relations campaigns to spread fear about military threats from foreign countries such as Iran, North Korea, China, Russia, and Venezuela. (*Z Magazine*, April 2007). A Defense News with the headline, "China, Iran top USA threat List," featured an interview with Air Force General T. Michael Moseley who argued that "these emerging threats require the nation to pay the price to modernize its fleet." (Z Magazine, April 2007). It is very interesting to note that many retired generals tend to be asked to serve on the board of directors of these corporations and use their influence with the Pentagon for military contracts.

Since the collapse of communism at the eve of the twentieth century (1989), Islamic terrorism has been the new demon in the west, in the U.S, in particular. Islamophobia has been promoted internationally as the new threat to western societies in general and Christianity in particular to maintain, among other things, the military production. Military and political strategists ignored the fact that 1.3 billion Muslims around the globe are peaceful loving people. Instead, they focus on a fraction of 1 percent and use it as pretext to represent all Muslims as terrorists.

Even some Christian leaders referred to Islam as a religion of violence. Islamophobia in western societies has been functioning in cyclical fashion for the last thousand years. It started with the Crusades war during the 10th century, when Pope Benedict the Second called for the Crusades war to save Christ's land from the infidels. The irony of this call is the fact, that Christ's lands was shared by the followers of the monotheistic religions; Judaism, Christianity, and Islam. People in that region of the world coexisted in harmony with one another.

Politicians and some religious leaders have used Islamophobia to further their own personal agendas. President Bush himself referred to the Iraqi invasion as a crusader's war but later, apologized for misusing that phrase.

President Barack Obama started a new mission with the hope of repairing the damage caused by the Bush administration, especially in the arena of American foreign policy. His visit to Egypt on June 4, 2009, to address the Muslim world is a gesture to establish a new, peaceful trend between the U.S. and the Arab world in particular and Islam in general. In his speech, President Obama used the term "extremist Muslim" instead "Islamic terrorism." Unfortunately, his speech turned out to be a public relations message to the Egyptian people in particular and the Muslim world in general. American foreign policy in the Middle East continued to proceed on the same path.

Another trend that began with President Obama is reflected in the military and defense budget. Secretary of Defense Robert Gates spoke on Capitol Hill in January 2009 and told lawmakers "tough choices" lay ahead for military spending and growing competition for domestic dollars. Gates said this meant "the spigot of defense funding opened by 9/11 in closing PDF." The U.S. spent a staggering $696 billion on defense in 2008: the largest defense budget since World War II."[16]

President Eisenhower's farewell address to the nation more than five decades ago warning the nation of the influence and abuse of the American military-industrial complex is as valid today as it was then. One sentence in particular should be emphasized for the benefit of the younger American generation and the readers at large:

"In the affairs of government, we must guard against the acquisition of unwarranted influence, whether sought or unsought, by the military-industrial complex."

---

[16] *New York Times* (Feb/27/09)

Economic and Human Costs

President Bush's tragic invasion of Iraq brought many negative consequences, especially for the U.S. and for Iraq. The U.S. has experienced a massive economic burden as a result of the cost of the war, which has already impacted the national economy. Bush borrowed heavily, especially from China, to pay for a war at a cost of one million dollars per minute. Unfortunately, the younger future American generation will assume that heavy economic burden that Bush created. During his eight years as president, the U.S. foreign debt more than doubled, increasing from $5 trillion to $10 trillion.

Another terrible and unforgivable consequence of the war is the human suffering. How could Bush and his administration push for an unnecessary war to justify the deaths of more than 4,500 American soldiers? As usual, his answers to those who have lost a loved one is that they died defending their country—fighting in a war that was based on fabricated lies and manipulated intelligence reports to mislead the American people and justify the invasion of Iraq.

According to the New York Times, Vice President Joe Biden paid a visit to Iraq on July 4, 2009 to address the troops. He noted that the troops were going home, as promised by President Obama, as well as the terrible cost of the Bush's war: 4,500 troops killed, more than 36,000 wounded, and more than 17,000 critically injured.

The economic burden of Bush's war has been analyzed by prominent scholars. Dr. Joseph Stiglitz, and Dr. Linda J. Bilmes, both economists, noted in their article: "The $10 Trillion Hangover: Paying the price for eight years of Bush." They pointed out that, "In the eight years since Bush took office, nearly every component of the U.S. economically has deteriorated. The nation's budget deficit, trade deficits, and debt have reached record levels. Unemployment and inflation are up, and household savings are down. Nearly, 4 million manufacturing jobs have disappeared and not coincidentally, 5 million more Americans do not have health insurance. Consumer debt has almost doubled, and nearly one fifth of American homeowners are likely to owe in mortgage debt than their homes are actually worth. Meanwhile, as we have reported previously, the final price for the war in Iraq is expected to reach at least $3 trillion. By using conservative assumptions, we calculate that the bill for Bush-era excess – the total new debt combined with the total new accrued obligation amounts to $10.35 trillion. This legacy will have long term consequence for America's prosperity, but it also will weigh heavily and immediately on the Obama administration, which will need to spend money quickly to get the economy moving again."[17]

Since this report was published, the economic meltdown has been exacerbated and several more million people have lost their jobs. In addition, Bush's Iraq war was still going on when his second term ended in 2008. The Iraq war also opened the door for corruption and the manipulation of the system in the U.S., as well as in Iraq. Billions of dollars of American taxpayers' money, as well as Iraqi oil money, disappeared without accountability. American and Iraqi contractors dipped their hands into public funds to perform projects that they have contracted, but many were poorly finished or never initiated.

According to the New York Times article ,"The Fog of Accountability," oil revenues (363 tons of cash) were bundled up and flown to Baghdad on 484 pallets from the Federal Reserve Bank to begin a new Iraqi government. In addition, " … the special inspector general for Iraqi reconstruction reported that $8.8 billion of the cash surge could not be adequately accounted for …"

The article goes on to say, "… Mr. [Paul] Bremer's provisional authority, with the full backing of the White House and the Pentagon, doled out an estimated $12 billion to dodgy ministries …" In addition to the Iraqi money, which disappeared without accountability, American taxpayers have also been the target of fraud and abuse.

Furthermore, the New York Times (8/13/2008) reported, "According to congressional budget office, the U.S. government spent over $100 billion between 2003 and 2008 on contractors for services in support of the war and reconstruction. Senator Byron Dorgan recently proposed the creation of a special committee in the U.S. Senate to exercise oversight over contracting abuses related to re-construction and the war in Iraq and Afghanistan."[18] The mass media in the U.S. continued to focus on U.S. government officials and contractor corruption in Iraq.

 The New York Times reported (February 15, 2009), the federal authority examining the early, chaotic days of the $125 billion Americans led to rebuild Iraq has significantly broadened their inquiry to include senior American military officers who oversaw the program, according to interviews with senior government officials and court documents.

---

[17] Harper Magazine, (Jan. 2009)

[18] The **New York** Times (8/13/2008)

Officers oversaw the program, according to an interview with senior government officials and court documents. The New York Times continued to note, that prosecutors have won 35 convictions on cases related to reconstruction in Iraq, yet most of them involved private contractors or mid-level officials. The investigation, which is being conducted by the special inspector general of Iraq Reconstruction Justice Department, the Army's Criminal Investigation command, and other federal agencies cover a period when millions of dollars in cash, often in stacks of shrink wrapped bricks of $100 dollar bills were dispensed from a loosely guarded safe in the basement often of Saddam Hussein's former palaces."

The tragic aspect of America's corrupt policy in Iraq was discovered recently, and it goes back to 2003 when unethical practices were taking place on a wide scale. The New York Times reported (December 16, 2003) news stories about possible profiteering by Halliburton and other U.S. contractors in Iraq. The article continued to note, that Halliburton, Bechtel, and other major contractors have been investigated heavily in political influence, not just through campaign contributions, but by enriching people they believe might be helpful.

Dick Cheney is part of a long (if not exactly proud) tradition; Brown and Rost which later became the Halliburton subsidiary involved in those dubious deals in Iraq, profited handsomely from its early support of young politician named Lyndon Johnson.

What contributed to the difficulties of the investigation of corruption during the Bush administration is attributed to the Bush' administration's policy of secrecy across many critical operations of the federal government. Since 9/11, the administration has invoked national security to justify this secrecy.

Many leading newspapers reported on corruption in Iraq such as the Washington Post, the New York Times, and the LA Times from 2003 to 2011, but the response was meager. The New York Times noted (February 15, 2009) that: "You had no oversight, chaos and breathtaking sums of money, [sic]" said Senator Claire McCaskill, a Missouri Democrat who helped create the wartime contracting commission, an oversight board. "And overall of that was the notion that failure was OK, it doesn't get any better for criminals than that set of circumstances."

The large-scale corruption taking place during the Iraq war was also attributed to the lack of accountability on the part of the federal government and congress, who were under the thumb of lobbyists representing American corporations that were bankrupt form the war.

The Consequences of Depleted Uranium

There are other severe consequences of the Iraq war that caused serious health problems to American soldiers as well as the Iraqi people in general, which has been attributed to depleted uranium (DU). DU weaponry was used first during the 1991 Gulf War and used again during the 2003 Iraqi invasion. A large area in Iraq has been permanently contaminated with radiation. The Christian Science Monitor noted on February 20, 2002, that DU is made from nuclear waste material left over from making nuclear weapons and fuel. American gunners used 320 tons of it in 1991 to destroy 4,000 Iraqi armored vehicles and swiftly concluded victory.

"But," the article notes, "the invisible particles created when those bullets struck and burned are still 'hot.' They make Geiger counters sing and they stick to the tanks, contaminating the soil and blowing in the dessert wind, as they will for 4.5 billion years—the time it will take the DU to loose just half of its radioactivity."

The Monitor quoted Dr. Asaf Durakovic, a former chief of nuclear medicine at Veteran's Hospital and head of the private Uranium Medical Research Center, in the Peer Reviewed Journal, "Military Medicine" August 2001. Durakovic published the result that "14 of 27 ill Gulf War vets had DU in their urine nine years after the war." The U.S. Department of Veteran Affairs has already provided compensation for nearly one in four veterans. Furthermore, the article states, "Iraqis say DU is a major cause of the severe health problems such as cancer and birth defects that they graphically show are surging in southern Iraq, though they do not have the clinical capability to link DU to health problems."

Scientists studying the biological effects of uranium in the 1960s reported that, "it targets the DNA." Marion Fulk, a nuclear chemist retired from the Livermore Nuclear Weapons Lab and formerly involved with the Manhattan project, interprets the new and rapid malignancies in American soldiers from the 2003 war as "spectacular and a matter of concern."[19]

Truth Out, Issue (September 23, 2004) revealed that "Soldiers developing malignancies so quickly since 2003 can be expected to develop cancers from independent causes ... Medical experts report that this phenomenon of multiple malignancies from unrelated causes has been unknown until now and is a new syndrome associated with internal DU exposure." The article continued, "Not only were soldiers exposed to DU on and off the battlefields, but they brought it home ... In a group of 251 soldiers from a study group in Mississippi who had all had normal babies before the Gulf War, 67 percent of their post-war babies were born with severe birth defects."[1]

---

[19] Levren Moret. "Depleted Uranium Dirty Bombs, Dirty Missiles, Dirty Bullets." SF Bay View, September 23, 2004.

The American war machine that produced such dangerous weapons did not take into consideration its impact on American soldiers. Their major concern, as usual, was how effective such weapons would be in the battlefield.

Physical and Mental Disability

The impact of the "DU" on American soldiers who invaded Iraq reflects several negative physical consequences, including physical disabilities and psychological and emotional problems. For example, it has been reported that the suicide rate among the nation's active duty military personnel has spiked since 2012. Suicide rates of military personnel and combat veterans have risen sharply since 2005, when the war was intensifying. The report revealed that nearly one suicide was committed each day in 2012.

The multiple negative impacts of the wars in Iraq and Afghanistan were reflected in a report by Chris Adams (published in McClatchy Newspapers) titled "Mounting Toll of Iraq, Afghan Wars Could Soon Rival Vietnam." Adams pointed out that the data obtained under the Freedom of Information Act.

The interesting analysis of the wide range of U.S. veterans' physical and psychological problems as a result of the U.S. wars should be known to the American public at large. As a matter of fact, Adams encouraged writers and editors to use the McClatchy database to localize this story or to write their own stories.

The analysis is very pertinent to my investigation of the U.S. invasion of Iraq and I am grateful for Adams' efforts. The following is an excerpt from his report.

"The wars in Iraq and Afghanistan may be winding down, but the long-term costs of caring for those wounded in battle is on path to rival the costs of the Vietnam War.

While Vietnam extracted a far higher death toll — 58,000 compared with 6,300 so far in the war on terror — the number of documented disabilities from recent veterans is approaching the size of that earlier conflict, according to a McClatchy analysis of Department of Veterans Affairs data.

The data, obtained under the Freedom of Information Act and detailing all disability payments to veterans of all wars, show that veterans leaving the military in recent years are filing for and receiving compensation for more injuries than did their fathers and grandfathers.

At the same time, McClatchy found, the VA is losing ground in efforts to provide fast, efficient and accurate disability decisions. And the agency has yet to get control of a problem that has vexed it for years: The wide variation in disability payments by state and region, even for veterans with the same ailments.

For soldiers now coming home from Iraq and Afghanistan, this ongoing variation in an already-clogged disability system means the size of monthly compensation checks might be a quirk of geography.

Given the nature of today's disabilities, it's difficult to calculate how much it all might ultimately cost. "We're in somewhat uncharted waters," said Linda Bilmes, a Harvard University professor who has conducted an exhaustive study on the long-term costs of the wars.

Her most recent estimates, from 2010, indicate that providing disability payments to Iraq and Afghanistan war veterans could range from $355 billion to $534 billion over the next 40 years; on top of that, costs to the VA's medical system could range from $201 billion to $348 billion to treat veterans of the current wars.

For the VA system, that means costs will grow for years to come — even as the country is entering a period of belt-tightening that could reduce the size of government and put a damper on the agency's ability to find the money to pay these expenses.

The fatalities in war are only a small portion of its ultimate human cost. Soldiers back from the war in Afghanistan, which began in 2001, or the war in Iraq, which began in 2003, carry with them a lifetime of physical and mental reminders.

According to VA and Department of Defense information compiled by the advocacy group Veterans for Common Sense, 2.2 million service members have deployed to one of the wars since Sept. 11, 2001; 942,000 have deployed two or more times.

Of those, 6,300 service members have died, and 46,000 have suffered non-fatal wounds in action. But more than 600,000 veterans have filed for VA disability benefits, and more than 700,000 have been treated in the VA's medical system.

"Right now, VA is getting about 10,000 new Iraq and Afghanistan claims and patients per month," said Paul Sullivan, executive director of the National Organization of Veterans' Advocates, which helps veterans file their disability claims. "The numbers are devastating."

Compensating veterans for those injuries is the duty of the VA. The department has long been guided by the words of President Abraham Lincoln, who vowed "to care for him who shall have borne the battle, and for his widow and his orphan."[20]

---

[20]Adams, Chris. "Mounting Toll of Iraq, Afghan Wars Could Soon Rival Vietnam." McClatchy DC. December 5, 2011.

For more information on the effects of DU on health and the environment check the following sources:

1. Depleted uranium: Dirty Bombs, Dirty Missiles, Dirty Bullets by L. Moret2. Discounted casualties: The Human Cost of Nuclear War" by Akira Tashiro, followed by L. Moret
2. L. Moret, Depleted Uranium: the Trojan Horse of Nuclear War" World Affairs Journal (8/2004)
3. Christopher Bollyn: Depleted Uranium; US Commits War Crime against Iraq, Humanity" (Part I)
4. Cancer Epidemic caused by US. WMD: MD says depleted uranium Linked" (Part II), American Free
5. Press, Four Part Series on DU (Truth Out, 9/23/2004)

5. www.nytimes.com/2012/06/09

Chapter V: Consequences of the War on the Iraqi Society

Iraq's society is historically known as the land between the two rivers, the Tigris and Euphrates. It is also known as the birthplace of civilization, which began more than five thousand years ago. It is an area where the Mesopotamian kingdoms of Sumer, Akkad and Babylon flourished for thousands of years. With the rise of Islam during the seventh century A.D., Baghdad was the center of learning, which lasted until the middle of the 13th century and led to the rise of Arab-Islamic civilization. In 1258, the Arab-Islamic Empire was invaded by an Asiatic tribe, the Mongols, who destroyed the basic infrastructure, such as system of irrigation and burned libraries, and learning institutions.

The invasion weakened the Arab-Islamic Empire, which later led to the rise of the Ottoman Emire. This empire dominated the region until the end of World War I in 1918.

History has been shown to repeat itself. The American invasion on March 19, 2003 left a large scale of destruction of the basic infrastructures, including electric power, water network, and sewage system; even some academic and historical archives did not escape destruction. The Iraqi National Museum was looted of more than 15,000 historical artifacts while American troops were watching. The only important government institution that was kept intact was the ministry of oil. After all, that was one of the main reasons behind the invasion of Iraq.

The invasion has negatively impacted every segment of the society, as well as its political, economic, physical, moral and cultural characteristics. Shedding light on some of these will reflect on Bush's war atrocities, which the majority of the American media has ignored.

Human Causalities

The majority of the American population is not aware of the high number of Iraqis who have been killed since the invasion in 2003. During the beginning of the war, Secretary of Defense Ronald Rumsfeld was asked publicly about Iraqi casualties, his response was, "We don't keep statistics on those who have died in Iraq." Rumsfeld considered Iraqis as war collateral damage and insignificant to him. Also, the American media ignored the Iraqi casualties but they shed light on the number of American soldiers who have been killed.

Extra Journal (January/February, 2008) referred to two research projects: "The Johns Hopkins School of Public Health, published in the prestigious British medical journal, the Lancet (October 21, 2006), and the other released by the British polling firm Opinion Research Business (September 2007). Both indicate that over a million Iraqis have been killed. Yet, an Associated Press poll

(February 24, 2007) asking Americans how many Iraqis have died received a median response of less than 10,000." John Hopkins updated research (September 28, 2007) on Iraqi deaths currently stands at 1.1 million killed. Again, in September 2007, the ORB released a poll finding that 1.2 million Iraqis have been violently killed since the U.S. invasion.

As FAIR Media has noted (March 21, 2007), Iraqi deaths have been ignored by the American media. However, in contrast to the statistics of death for example in Kosovo or Darfur, the American media tends to provide continuous and full coverage while death statistics of Iraqi causalities are reported, but the numbers tend to be much smaller and reported in "estimates."

The large number of Iraqis who have been killed since the 2003 invasion led to further tragic consequences. According to the New York Times (Febuary 23, 2009), it has been estimated that there are 740,000 Iraqi widows that survived their deceased husbands in Iraq. As the number of widows has swelled during eight years of war, their presence on the city streets, begging for food or as potential recruits by insurgents has become a vexing symbol of the breakdown of Iraqi self-sufficiency.

When Leila Kadim, a managing director in the Ministry of Labor and Social Affairs was asked about the Iraqi widows' tragedy, her response was, "There are too many." The New York Times article "Iraq's War Widows Face Dire Need With Little Aid" states, "Among Iraqi females aged 15-80, one in 11 are estimated to become widows … A United Nations report estimated that during the height of sectarian violence here in 2006, 90 to 100 women were widowed each day." The article also states, "In large cities like Baghdad, the presence of war widows is difficult to ignore. Cloaked in black abayas, they wade through columns of cars idling at security checkpoints, asking for money or food. They wait in line outside mosques for free blankets, or sift through mounds of garbage piled along the street. Some live with their children in public parks or inside gas station restrooms."

According to the Iraqi government, roughly, one in six widows receives state aid. The BBC article "The shame of Iraq's pariah widows" states, "Widows were supposed to be given just over $1.00 a day from the government. But a survey by the charity, Oxfam, has discovered that less than a quarter actually receive the money." The article noted that 40 percent of all prostitutes in Iraq are widows. Many of these women are responsible for supporting their children, parents and other members of their family as a result of the death of a husband, a father or a brother.

In 2008, the pace of the aggression began to slow down. However, it is still difficult to assess the extent of damage caused by the invasion. A true evaluation of the destruction could be accomplished only years after the war ended. Nevertheless, two recent studies have been released by the Iraqi government and the World Health Organization on mental conditions as a result of the war.

According to the New York Times article "Iraqi Surveys Start to Unveil the Mental Scars of War, Especially Among Women" by Alissa Rubin, "… the Iraqi government and the World Health Organization surveyed 4,332 Iraqis over 18 years old nationwide and found that 17 percent suffered from mental disorders of some kind, with depression, phobias, post-traumatic stress disorder and anxiety among the most common." The article also noted "The survey found that more than three-quarters of all widows were not receiving pensions, and a third of the women surveyed had three hours or less electricity per day. Quality health care is harder to obtain than it was in 2006 and 2007, they said."

The article quoted Olga Ghazaryan, Oxfam's regional director for the Middle East. "'These widows take care not only of their children but often of their extended family so they are bearing a heavy burden," Ms. Ghazaryan said. 'The responsibility of finding food for the family and obtaining electricity and water puts great stress on women.'"

During Bush's last trip to Iraq (December 2009) inside the green zone, at a press conference, an Iraqi journalist, Muntathar al-Zeida threw his shoes at the president. The first that he threw at President Bush, he shouted, "This is a message of retaliation on behalf of the widows of Iraq." The second shoe he threw, he shouted, "This is on behalf of the orphans of Iraq." The biggest insult to a person according to Arab culture is to hit a person with a shoe.

Mr. Al-Zeidi, within a few hours after the incident, was on television, which turned him into a legend and hero in the eyes of hundreds of millions of people in the Arab world in particular and the rest of the world in general. Some wealthy individuals in the Gulf area offered millions of dollars for the pair of shoes, which were destroyed by the Iraqi authorities.

Mr. Al-Zeida is an investigative journalist who was well aware of the tragic life the Iraqi widows and orphans were experiencing on a daily basis. The British newspaper, The Guardian (April 6, 2009) noted that, "Iraqi babies for sale: people trafficking crisis grows as gangs exploit poor families and corrupt system: the article referred to a senior police officer who said at least 15 Iraqi children were sold every month at a rate between £200 and £4000 per child, some overseas, some internally, some for adoption, and some for sexual abuse. The reporter interviewed Sarah Taminn, 38, a widow and mother of five from Babel, said she had already sold children ages four and two in the past year. She is living in a displacement camp without a job or support. "I love all my children; I know that the families who adopted them will give them a good life, food, and an education that I could never give."

DU and its impact

Since the American invasion of Iraq in 2003, the dropping of bombs is having a drastic impact on the Iraqi population and its physical environment.

It has been reported (Aljazeera, 9/1/2009) that the number of children born with physical defects in Iraq has been increasing. This is the beginning of a human tragedy for many future Iraqi generations, due to the biological effect of DU.

It is also unfortunate that the DU caused by American dirty bombs dropped from the air and bombs used during the 1991 Gulf invasion and the 2003 invasion of Iraq is causing irreparable damage, not only to the Iraqi people, but also to many American soldiers who were close to contaminated areas in Iraq, as indicated in the previous chapter.

During the past few years, there have been few attempts to investigate the impact of DU on the Iraqi people and their physical environment. I published a post about this subject on my blog "Middle East Today" on November 15, 2009.

"The depleted uranium (DU) found in Iraq, especially in Felluja, was a fallout from the bombs used both times during the 1991 Gulf War, and during the 2003 Iraqi invasion. The impact on the Iraqi people as well as the American soldiers has been disastrous.

The Felluja people have witnessed ferocious battles between American forces and Iraqi insurgent groups.

The Christian Science Monitor (2/20/02) noted that DU "is made from nuclear waste material and fuel. The American army used 320 tons in 1991 to destroy 4,000 Iraqi armored vehicles and swiftly concluded victory."

The Guardian newspaper (11/14/09) reported that babies born with physical defects in Felluja increased by fifteen folds. This, according to British and Iraqi medical team, is due to poisonous chemicals such as DU.

Recently, Al Jazeera.net (10/30/09) stated that it has received a copy of a report written by physicians and scientists that was sent to the United Nations. The report confirmed that the number of babies born in Felluja in September 2009 was 170. Twenty four per cent of them died within a week of their birth, and 75% were born with physical defects. These figures were compared with the number of birth, in Felluja, during August 2002, which was 530, only 6 babies died within the first week after their birth, and one baby was born with physical defect.

Furthermore, in the report, the British and Iraqi medical team requested from the United Nations to investigate the high percentage of newly born babies with physical defects, and the possibility of war crimes committed by the invading forces.

It should be noted here that many American veterans have also been physically affected due to their contact with depleted uranium.

Would this report be seriously considered by the United Nations? This remains to be seen. Meanwhile the consequences of the war are going to be felt by the Iraqi people, and young American veterans for many more years to come."[21]

Infrastructure Destruction

The basic infrastructure in Iraq was destroyed by aerial bombardment during the invasion by American forces. It has been acknowledged that more bombs were dropped on Baghdad than on Berlin during World War II. This destruction impacted electrical power facilities, water purification system and the sewage system as well. Despite the billions of dollars spent so far to repair and reconstruct the basic infrastructure the system still operates below 50% of its capacity prior to the invasion (March 19, 2003).

More than 70% of the population is not receiving safe potable drinking water. Water resources are polluted due to the dysfunctional sewage system, especially in big cities such as Baghdad and Basra in the South. Electrical power is also operating at a lower rate and consumers are getting power supply on a limited basis. The insufficient production of electrical power and the shortage of fresh clean water for consumption increase the risk of illness and disease.

The wide range of destruction and its impact on the Iraqi population was summarized in a presentation by Dr. Omar Al-Kubaisy's to the members of the European parliament on March 20, 2009 in Arabic and translated to English by Imad Khadduri.

---

[21] The research was conducted by a non-profit research group, Oxfam and Amal, the focus of their research on issues of concern to women.

However, suffice it to say, this is a country where:

- 70% of its doctors have emigrated.

- More than 5,500 of its scientist and academics have been killed or imprisoned or have emigrated.

- 70% of its hospitals have minimum standard performance, below the required standards in the remnants of what is destroyed, raided, or stolen.

- 90% of medicines in pharmacies are either analyzed or not registered or is contaminated. These medications are bought on the black market across the borders by ghost companies and given out by thousands of unlicensed pharmacies and drug depots run by people who are not pharmacists.

- Its hospitals are used as centers for ethnic and sectarian physical liquidation and terror by the militias.

- The Ministry of Health is part of a sectarian quota division system that specifies the identity of the minister and the directors general and is controlled by the theocratic political parties as well as the religious and sectarian militias. It is an institution in which financial and administrative corruption prevails and according to the Transparency Committee, more than 2 billion U.S. dollars have disappeared as a result of phony ghost contracts and bribery.

- There is no supervisory or monitoring role to be mentioned by the present parliamentarians who are doctors, but on the contrary, their interference may cause a negative effect on the size and the nature of the financial and administrative corruption.

- There is widespread mental illness and drug addiction and the widespread growth of opium poppy plantations and opium for the first time since the occupation.

- Alteration of basic medical purchase requirements and their replacement with insignificant lists and invoices.

- The spread of epidemics and the loss of credibility of all statistics and the lack of statistics of cholera, measles, diphtheria, and whooping cough, and toxoplasmosis and a worsening of tuberculosis and HIV/AIDS.

- Unsafe, imported foods.

- A rise of incidences in cancer and the nature of the registered cases recently and a rise in cases of congenital malformation as due to the aggravate complications as a result of radioactive pollution and the burning down of trees. Pollution of rivers, as result of the collapse of the sewage system, particularly in the Middle and the South caused by the use of DU and White Phosphorous as well as Cluster Bombs and the prevention by the occupation forces of remedial measures and surveys to discover the polluted locations for sterilization and cleansing.

- The proliferation of landmines in the sites of the old wars, as well as unexploded ordinance, especially in Basra and in border areas.

- Loss of cooperation and harmony with the humanitarian and voluntary organizations, such as the Red Cross and Red Crescent Societies and others, as well as financial corruption in the Iraqi Red Crescent Society, and the escape of its president outside of Iraq with U.S. protection.

- Lack of medicines and supplies and as well as minimal financial allocations, since they did not exceed 4% of the overall budget allocations in the best of cases, and because of rampant corruption.

- Lack of safe potable water for more than 70% of the population and the continuing lack of electricity as well as the lack of proper sanitation.

- The highest rates of infant and newborn mortality in the world.

In Iraq after the occupation:

- More than five million are displaced and more than 4 million are below poverty level.

- Approximately two million widows.

- Five million orphans

- Insufficient food for more than eight million

- More than 400,000 have been detainees and prisoned.

- More than 28% of the population is unemployed.[22]

---

[22] Imad Khadduri, http://Abutamam.blogspot.com

The Iraqi Industry

Another economic sector that also did not escape the aftermath of the American

invasion is the Iraqi industry, prior to the U.N. embargo after the first Gulf War of 1991 and the second war of 2003, which expanded at a rapid rate and employed more than half a million workers. However, the wars have changed the industrial sector, through direct and indirect policies that were initiated by the occupying American forces.

The Washington Post (May 14, 2007) stated that according to Paul Brinkley, a deputy undersecretary of defense, advocated to rehabilitate shattered state-run enterprises to employ tens of thousands of Iraqis who are unemployed to reduce violence. According to the World Bank, 192 state-owned factories employed more than 500,000 people before the war. But, the U.S. occupation administrator, L. Paul Bremer, deemed government socialism to be a bad economic policy. He wanted private industries to buy the factories.

The factories remained shuttered, some workers found new jobs and others left. The U.S. military officials believe that many of the unemployed joined the insurgency. The article noted that the Pentagon's civilian leadership, dominated by Neo-Cons, rejected the idea of supporting government run-industry. Furthermore, P. Bremer issued an order in 2004, which prevents the Iraqi Central Bank from funding state-owned enterprise despite the fact according to Brinkley that underemployed and unemployed Iraqis may approach 70 percent.

Bremer's political strategy largely backfired and added to Iraq's turmoil and violence. Furthermore, his reckless policy played into the hands of Iraqi extremists and to other people in the Arab world. Bremer's policy was enforced after the U.S. occupation was no surprise to the people who were aware of his background as a Neo-Con and an associate of Henry Kissinger.

From day one, Bremer's intention toward Iraq was not a positive one. He must have learned a lesson from the previous Secretary of State, Kissinger, because when he was asked about the Iraqi-Iranian War during 1980s, his response then was, "Let both sides bleed themselves to death and this is the best scenario for the West."

The Iraqi Army

Bremer's policy in Iraq created the image that the US is not only an occupying military force, but also a Neo-Con colonist strategy. Iraq has experienced British colonialism during 1920s-1930s, which led at the time to the Iraqi revolution against British occupying forces. Iraqis view the U.S. occupation as a form of neo-colonization, dismantling both the Iraqi army and the civil service cadre as a step toward de-Ba'athification was a clear policy of Neo-

Colonization. Furthermore, the destruction of the Iraqi army was part of the neo-con strategy to benefit and strengthen Israel's defense forces. The Iraqi army was the second strongest military force after the Egyptian army.

Bremer's reckless policy led many of those who have lost their source of economic support from the disbanded Iraq army of more than 400,000 soldiers and the de-ba'athificaton of the civil service to join the insurgency movement. General John Abu-Zaid, commanding American forces in the Middle East at that time, stated publicly that the number of al-Qaeda –the followers of abu-Musad al-Zarqawi were no more than 4-5% of the insurgency. The rest are members from the dissolved army and the Ba'ath party.

The Ba'ath party included Sunnis, Shiites and Kurds. It was a secular political ideology. Those who joined the insurgency came from the three sectarian groups. Immediately after the invasion, a list of the most wanted high ranking officials in Saddam Hussein's government. The list was reflected as a deck of cards: fifty-two individuals as the most wanted criminals.

The deck of cards reflected the officials who were wanted by the occupation authority starting with Saddam Hussein and his two sons. The interesting part of the deck of cards is that thirty-seven of those high officials were Shiites. This reflects an important policy that despite the fact that Saddam was ruthless dictator who butchered many Iraqis especially from various religious groups, his regime was the most secular in the Middle East region.

At an international conference on economic development in Iraq which was held in Amman, Jordan on March 13, 2009, the Iraqi vice president, Tariq al-Hashimi in his presentation said, "The American invasion of Iraq produced tragic and negative consequences to the Iraqi economy. The destruction of industrial factories, theft and decline in productivity of more than 192 large public economic establishments, in addition, to more than 60,000 private industrial projects. The open-door economic policy, which was initiated by the occupying forces, led to the flooding of imported cheap products, which also made it difficult for what was left by the public industrial sector to compete." He also said that the rate of inflation exceeds 14 percent according to the Iraqi Central Bank and the unemployment rate, according to government estimates, was 15 percent, but it is worsening due to the declining oil prices globally. Al-Hashimi stated, "Due to unstable conditions, foreign investors will not take the risk to participate in the economic development in Iraq."[23]

During an interview with Dr. Abed al-Musain Zeidan, who is in charge of economic planning at the Ministry of Planning, he stated, "Iraq needs at least $100 billion to rebuild it's infrastructure and economy, which will require at least

---

[23] For more information on the economic conference check: http://www.al-jazeera.net (3/13/2009)

five years. The required investment is to revitalize the industrial and agricultural sectors." He continued to say, "Both major sectors of the economy had been paralyzed. However, the agriculture sector is better than the industrial and still employs 40% of the labor force and contributes 30% to the national economy."[24]

From 2007 - 2009, the agricultural sector started experiencing difficulty due to drought and the decreasing flow of water in both rivers, the Euphrates and Tigris (Dijlah). Both rivers originate in Turkey. The Turkish government has been building many dams during the past three decades and the end result of that will be negative for both Iraq and Syria. The consequences of the American invasion affected all sectors of the Iraqi economy and destroyed the economic progress that was accomplished during the previous three decades.

Iraqi Refugees

Another troubling consequence of the Iraq invasion is reflected in the huge number of people who fled their country for safety reasons. The sectarian civil war and the bombardment of neighborhoods by the occupying forces led to the killing of more than 1.2 million Iraqis. According to the U.N. Refugee Agency, more than four million Iraqis have been displaced from their homes due to violence and threat of the sectarian war. The spokeswoman for the agency, Jennifer Bagonese, released figures to the press in Geneva, Switzerland stating that the number of Iraqi refugees who fled from Iraq was estimated at 2.2 million. Another 2 million were displaced from their homes and moved into other areas in Iraq and neighboring Arab-countries for safety. Furthermore, she continued to say that Syria is hosting nearly 1.4 million Iraqis refugees and Jordan around 750,000. Such a huge number created a heavy economic burden on both Syria and Jordan. The internal movement in Iraq also created human agony. She noted that the influx of Iraqi refugees into neighboring Arab countries created economic hardship for all. Further evidence revealed that European countries admitted thousands Iraqis, especially in the Scandinavian countries. The irony of this tragedy, caused by the Bush's administration, is that the U.S. government accepted only a few thousand Iraqi refugees in 2007.[25]

The tragedy of the Iraqi refugees and their economic conditions has reached an unbearable level. Many of them have spent their liquid assets, which they brought with them to Syria and Jordan. The economic hardship in both Syria and Jordan makes it impossible to find jobs. According to the Christian Science Monitor (April 12, 2009), 4.7 million Iraqis left their homes since the war began, up from 3.8 million two years ago. To ease the economic burden on Syria and

---

[24] www.aljazeera.net (3/13/2009). For more information, visit www.aljazeera.net (8/21/2007)

[25] www.aljazeera.net (6/6/2007)

Jordan, the Obama administration announced additional funds for displaced Iraqis, bringing the U.S. commitment for the year 2009 to roughly $150 million. In 2008, the U.S. contributed $400 million." Six years after the invasion that turned the country into a battleground, sectarian civil war, suicide bombings, and kidnappings are the major cause behind the influx of refugees out of Iraq.

How soon these refugees will be able to return to their homes is, as of yet, unknown, and the strife among Sunni, Shiites and Kurds is ongoing. The aftermath of the Iraqi war also led to the deterioration of nearly all private and public services. According to the World Health Organization, health care services in Iraq have been deteriorating badly due to the shortage of physicians, medical equipment, and medicine.[1]

According to the spokeswoman of the U.N. Health Organization, Fadelah al-Shaib, more than 70% of patients who were injured in the war die in the hospitals due to shortage of medicine and medical personnel. She continued to say that the general health condition of the poor Iraqi population is very bad. 80% of them have no hygiene facilities due to the destruction of the public sewage system and 70% are unable to get fresh clean water to drink.

Furthermore, 60 percent were only able to get food subsidies from charitable organizations. UNICEF also revealed in 2006 that premature deaths among children under the age of five was estimated at one third and 21% are suffering from malnutrition.[26]

This human agony in Iraq has been also confirmed by a report published by an American organization, called "Rescue the Children," which notes that infant mortality rates among Iraqis is the highest in the world. 122,000 children under the age of five years old died in 2006-2007, half of them during the first month of birth. A number of factors contributed to such high infant mortality, including lack of health care, shortage of clean drinking water, shortage of electrical power, poverty, and hardship of life to too many people."

The Iraqi health condition has been on the decline since the economic embargo imposed on Iraq by the U.S. through the U.N. Between 1991-2003, more than 500,000 Iraqi children died unnecessarily. Madeleine Albright, the Secretary of State during the Clinton administration was asked about the economic embargo and its impact on the deaths of more than half a million Iraqi children. Her response was, "Blame Saddam Hussein for it."[27] Some politicians have lost their human compassion and the deaths of innocent children mean nothing to them.[28]

---

[26] www.aljazeera.net-/Templates/postings/pocket pc detailed page, aspx (4/22/2007)

[27] www.aljazeera.net-/Templates/postings/pocket pc detailed page, aspx

The April 2007 Reuters article "Humanitarian situation in Iraq worsening: Red Cross" states, "The suffering of Iraqi civilians is worsening and there is no sign yet that a security crackdown in Baghdad is bringing relief, the International Committee of the Red Cross (ICRC) said." The article continued, "Hospitals were stretched to the limit by daily mass casualties, malnutrition was on the rise and power shortages were becoming more frequent around the country."

The Iraqi Academic Community and Terrorism

The invasion of Iraq has negatively impacted every aspect of life in Iraq. The academic community in general has experienced death and terror, and many fled the country to seek safety with their families.

Koichiro Malsuura, the Director General of UNESCO appealed (April 14, 2006) for international support to Iraqi academics and intellectuals and called for measures to protect them from a "heinous campaign of violence." According to the Center for the Arab and Mediterranean World, some 180 academics have been killed in Iraq between 2003 and 2006 and thousands more have been driven into exile.[29]

The problems of the Iraqi academic community were also revealed by a Los Angeles Times interview with Seeham Shoojairi, spokeswoman for the Iraqi Ministry of Higher Education. She stated, "Over 6,700 Iraqi academics left Iraq since the American invasion (March 19, 2003), and only 150 have returned back". She also stated, "More than 300 academics have been assassinated."[30] Furthermore, a prominent Iraqi, Shaick Harith Al-Thani, the head of the Learned Islamic Council, said that, "There is a heavy Israeli presence all over Iraqi. Some were in Kurdistan prior of the American invasion. Others came after the occupation of Iraq. Many of them are part of the American security forces. Also, there are others who are performing suspected secret roles under the umbrella of the U.S. occupation."[2]

It was no longer a secret in Iraq or the Arab world that Israeli forces were part of the American occupation forces. The Israeli newspaper Haaretz revealed that

(4/22/2007)

[28] www.aljazeera.net/Templates/postings/pocketpcdetailedpage,aspx (5/10/2007)

[29] www.Arabnews.com (4/15/2006)

[30] www.al-jazera.net (9/24/2008)

there are Israeli security companies are working with the U.S. forces in Iraq and that they brought advanced military equipment to give to Kurdish militias. Furthermore, the Haaretz also quoted the New Yorker Journal, stating that some of the Israeli soldiers are undercover and disguised as Iraqi individuals.

According to a study done by the Iraqi Babil House, many of the foreign security forces in Iraq are also Israeli and were accused of assassination of Iraqi academics. At an academic conference in Amman Jordan (July 19, 2007), the president of the Arab Universities Union, Dr. Saleh Hashim al-Amin warned that more than 4,000 Iraqi academics are no longer at their universities. More than 360 professionals and researchers have been assassinated. Another 3,500 fled the country. He continued to say that this intended campaign is to drain Iraq from its brainpower, which took many years to educate and train at a high financial cost. This is an intended policy that will lead to the destruction of Iraq.[31]

The previous Iraqi government encouraged many young people, males and females, to pursue higher education at the government's expense. Within three to four decades (1970s – 2000s) a high caliber of scientists and engineers acquired their education and training in Western academic institutions. That brainpower contributed a great deal to Iraq's economic development and scientific progress. One area of the major scientific research was the Iraqi nuclear research which Israel bombed in 1981. At that time, president Reagan condemned the Israeli aggression.

Furthermore, some of the Iraqi scientists who were involved in the area of nuclear research were assassinated, and the news among the Iraqi population was that the Israeli Mossad committed the killings. Another piece of evidence is also reflected in the assassination of an Egyptian nuclear scientist in Paris who, at the time, was working for the Iraqi government. The irony of history is reflected in our days, vis-à-vis Iran, which claims that one of their scientists was assassinated by the Israeli Mossad. In addition, the Israeli have threatened to bomb Iranian nuclear facilities. The ruthless Israeli policy, which played an important role in supporting the U.S. invasion of Iraq, boils down to a plain and fundamental Israel policy, which is "to be the only dominant nuclear military power in the region."

This puts Israel in a position to dictate its policy on various governments in the Middle East region, reflecting the concept, "might is right." Iraq was the most advanced country in the Arab world. It also possessed the basic ingredients for modernization: high educational attainment levels, the development of a rapid industrial and agricultural sectors, and huge natural resources such as oil.

---

[31] http://www.abram.org (7/19/2007)

Iraq ranks second in oil reserve, but that reserve might be triple according to some geological reports. Another important political factor is that the previous regime in Iraq was dominated by the Ba'ath party, which ideologically calls for Arab unity. All of these ingredients caused a panic in the minds of Israeli politicians; it was viewed as a potential future threat to Israeli's political and economic dominance of the region. The bombardment of a suspected nuclear facility in Syria (2007) fits this pattern. The present campaign against Iran reflects the aggressive Israeli policy, which also has been putting pressure on the previous Bush administration and the present administration to bomb Iran.

Conclusion

The invasion of Iraq by U.S. troops in 2003 lacked clear cause and noble purpose. It was a war by choice, not by necessity, and benefitted a few interest groups at the cost of the American national interest. It was a war based on planned false and deceptive reports used by George W. Bush and his corrupt political advisors and supporters to justify the invasion and mislead the American public.

It is regrettable to say that the invasion was not the first war the U.S. unjustly initiated, and it will probably not be the last one.

Military interferences by the U.S. in the internal affairs of foreign countries has been part of the U.S. government foreign policy through most of the country's history. However, this policy has increased since the end of the World War I.

In Robert Kagan's book, "The World America Made," the author writes, "The U.S. interfered militarily more than 29 times—or its military interference takes place once at least every 4 ½ years."

He continued to say that American military interferences took place in many geographical regions around the globe. As was reflected, the U.S. interference in the Middle East region in general and the Arab world in particular began at the end of World War II.[32]

The first blunder that was committed by President Harry Truman was the creation of the state of Israel in 1948, against the wishes of its Palestinian majority. This political interference led to the creation of a fascist state under the leadership of Zionist politicians who drove millions of Palestinians from their homes. This political policy, which, as of 2014, is still in practice and indirectly supported by the U.S, led not only to political instability, but also to the rise of international terrorism and the U.S. invasion of Iraq in 2003. As was reflected earlier, the Israeli supporters in the U.S. played the most influential role in supporting the invasion. George W. Bush admitted this when he stated publicly that the invasion of Iraq made Israel safer.

Furthermore, the September 11 terrorist attack against the Wrold Trade Center in New York city, which led to the deaths of nearly 4,000 innocent civilians, is the result of U.S. government interference in the internal affairs of Palestine in 1948.

---

[32] [1] Kagan, Robert. "The World America Made." Vintage Press, 2012

The majority of elected American politicians are corrupt because they put their own personal interests ahead of the U.S. national interest to ensure their political reelections. This is attributed mainly to the influence of financial political contributions from lobbyists and interest groups, who end up shaping the U.S. government policy at both the national and international levels.

The American public's view of its political representatives in congress has been negative for many years. Many surveys conducted over the past decade or more reflect a very negative image of the members of congress, which is reflected in their low approval ratings. A recent global survey conducted by "PEW Research" (2012) revealed that he U.S. image abroad in many regions was negative due to its interferences in the internal affairs of foreign states. Furthermore, the outcome of that survey also revealed that the majority of the American public is against the government interfering in foreign countries' national affairs. They are aware of the financial cost to fight foreign wars at the expense of American taxpayers. They are also aware of the fact that foreign debt more than doubled during Bush's unnecessary wars in Iraq and Afghanistan.

The American government's misguided foreign policy began to negatively imact the U.S. image globally. In a New York Times article (12/15/13), David Ignatius referred to the erosion of American power, based on Walter Russell Mead's essay "The End of History Ends." Ignatius wrote, "Mead warns that Obama's attempts to disengage from the over-commitments of George W. Bush's presidency have emboldened what he calls the central powers: Russia, China and Iran. With the United States in seeming retreat, these rivals think they have formed a way to challenge and ultimately to change the way global politics work."

In my judgment, President Obama's policy toward Iran's nuclear strategy is correct if it will be implemented. Israel played an influential political role in encouraging the U.S. to invade Iraq in 2003. Israel is the winner and the U.S. government is the loser.

The U.S. government left Iraq empty handed at a high economic and human cost.

Professor J. Stiglitz of Columbia University, and Professor L. Bilmes of Harvard University have estimated that the cost of the war in Iraq could reach between $2.5 and $3 trillion. Furthermore, Professor Stiglitz, a Nobel Prize winner and economist at Columbia University, pointed out that the invasion of Iraq in 2003 was the first war in U.S. history paid for entirely on credit card.

The reckless and irresponsible decision of Bush to go to war unnecessarily has caused a heavy physical, financial and social burden on American society. This is the tragedy of the Bush administration's fabrication of reports, which they used to mislead the American public to gain support for the war. The previous president should be tried for crimes committed, according to international law.

Furthermore, the American congress should also be blamed for giving Bush the green light to invade Iraq. The majority of its members have failed to investigate the secret reports that the president used to justify the invasion of Iraq. The president lied and misled the American people by using fabricated secret reports that Saddam Hussein possessed WMD and posted a threat to the security of the U.S.

It is unfortunate to say that the majority of the members of congress are influenced by lobbyists who represent big corporations and interest groups. In this case, lobbyists representing the military industrial complex have supported the Iraq invasion. In a war situation, the military and defense contracts enhance the margin of their profit. Also, the American oil companies were eager to get into the Iraqi oil fields because Iraq's oil reserve is the largest in the world. Other lobbyist groups connected with the neocons, such as AIPAC, have played a role in supporting the invasion for the benefit of Israel.

It is unfortunate to point out that the prevailing attitude among many members of congress is to be reelected. The lobbyists, whose numbers were estimated to exceed 16,000, are the major contributors to their political campaigns. In this case, I would say personally that this type of money is a source of evil and political corruption.

The tragedy of the invasion of Iraq and its aftermath brought many negative consequences to both the Iraqi and the American societies. It was the longest war that the U.S. has been involved in. Also, the impact of the war on Iraq is beyond the imagination of the average American citizen. The destruction of the Iraqi society politically, economically, physically and environmentally is difficult to explain.

Dahr Jamail, an international journalist, wrote a brief description of the negative impact of war in the Iraqi society. He stated, "Seventy two months of occupation with over $607 billion spent on the war by conservative estimates has resulted in 2.2 million internally displaced Iraqis, 2.7 million refugees 2,615 professors, scientists, and physicians killed in cold blood, and 338 dead journalists. Over $13 billion was misplaced by the current Iraqi government and another $400 billion is required to rebuild the Iraqi infrastructure. Unemployment fluctuates between 25 and 70%, depending upon the month. There are 24 car bombs per month, 10,000 cases of cholera per year, 4,261 dead U.S. soldiers, and over 70,000 physically or psychologically wounded soldiers."

According to Mr. D. Jamail, the film, "Iraq in Fragments" by James Longley, which was nominated for Best Documentary at the 2007 Academy Awards, best describes Iraq today. The country has been destroyed by decades of U.S. policy that has plagued Iraqis. Looking back only to the 1980s, we see George W. Bush's war against Iraq and Bill Clinton's and George W. Bush's oversight of 12 and a half years of genocidal and economic sanctions that killed half a million Iraqi children as a result of the 1991 Gulf invasion.

Today, under President Barack Obama, what is left of Iraq smolders in ruins. Obama ended the war and evacuated U.S. troops from the country in 2011, but economic and political corruption remain. In addition, Iraq's destruction of physical environment continues as a result of the explosive weapons enriched by DU.

Another, major blunder of George W. Bush's Iraq war is that he provided a golden opportunity to Iran to dominate the Iraqi political stage and indirectly control its present and future agendas. In a recent interview with Al-Ahram Newspaper (May 16, 2009), Mr. Mahmoud Al-Mashhadani, the previous president of the Iraqi parliament and chairman of the Iraqi national movement, stated, "The U.S. occupation of Iraq is an overt open and known policy, but the Iranian occupation of Iraq is a covert and secret policy." He warned the Arab world of Iranian penetrating influence in the region.

There are no doubts in my mind and the minds of other political analysts that George W. Bush and his administration formulated their strategy for the invasion of Iraq well in advance of 9/11. In the New York Times article "Yes He Would," Paul Krugman, the 2008 Nobel Prize winner noted, "First, it's clearer than ever that Mr. Bush, who still claims that war with Iraq was a last resort, was actually spoiling for a fight. The New York Times has confirmed the authenticity of a British government memo reporting on a prewar discussion between Mr. Bush and Tony Blair. In that conversation, Mr. Bush told Mr. Blair that he was determined to invade Iraq even if U.N. inspectors came up empty-handed."

---

* Dahr Jamail ("Foreign Policy in Focus," 4/12/09) has reported from inside Iraq and is the author of Beyond the Green Zone. He writes for inter press service, The Asia Times, and is a contributor to foreign policy in focus.

Mr. Krugman continued, "Second, it's becoming increasingly clear that Mr. Bush knew that the case he was presenting for war - a case that depended crucially on visions of mushroom clouds - rested on suspect evidence. For example, in the 2003 State of the Union address Mr. Bush cited Iraq's purchase of aluminum tubes as clear evidence that Saddam was trying to acquire a nuclear arsenal. Yet Murray Waas of the National Journal reports that Mr. Bush had been warned that many intelligence analysts disagreed with that assessment."

The two main sources that the Bush administration relied heavily on were based on the fabricated false reports provided by two Iraqis in exile. Both men, Ahmed Chalabi and Rafid Ahmad Alwa are known as felons and embezzlers. Ahmed

Chalabi has been tried in abstentia in Jordanian court for stealing money from a bank. He fled Jordan and he is still on the wanted list to serve a jail sentence.

In the U.S., he was known as the organizer of an Iraqi government in exile and was subsidized by the U.S. State Department at the rate of $3.5 million. Chalabi was unable to account for most of the money given to him and his financial support from the State Department stopped.

He was then recruited by the Neo-Cons to work for the Defense Department. He was close to both Paul Wolfowitz and Douglas Feith and began to provide them with false information about Iraq's WMD. How authentic the information he provided was irrelevant to both men because it supported their agendas. Mr. Ahmad Chalabi was also on the payroll of the Defense Department.

Mr. Chalabi served as an important source of phony information to Judy Miller, who is known as "WMD" expert. Her articles in the New York Times prior to the invasion focused on Saddam Hussein's dangerous WMD. When she was asked about the source of her information, she declined by saying, "I am not at liberty to reveal the source." The source was Chalabi—this felon will be ready to sing to any tone of music, as long as he gets paid for it.

The second source was Rafid Ahmad Alwan, who was living in Germany and was described by German intelligence as a "felon, a liar, heavy drinker, who had a mental break down." The German Intelligence also thinks he is a "fabricator."[1]

Mr. Alwan provided the fabricated report about the Mobil Chemical labs which Secretary of State, Collin Powell presented at the U.N. (February 15, 2003) as supporting evidence for the invasion of Iraq. This report, which was used by the Secretary of State, is referred to as the "Curveball Report"[33] by the German intelligence. The conspiracy for the invasion of Iraq, which began before 9/11, is no longer a secret. President Bush and his aides were fabricating intelligence reports to support the invasion of the Iraq in order to implement their hidden agenda.

The blunders committed by George W. Bush, Dick Cheney, Donald Rumsfeld and their high-ranking Neo-Con aides and advisors caused tremendous human political, economic and physical damage nationally and internationally, for which they should be held accountable.

At a public appearance on November 8, 1993, during his first campaign for governor, George W. Bush said, "I believe everybody should be held responsible

---

[33] For more information on the "Curveball" False Report see: Vincent Bugliosi, the Prosecution of George W. Bush for Murder. (Chapter 4)

for their own personal behavior. All public policy should revolve around the principle that individuals are responsible for what they say and do."[34]

Based on his own political philosophy, George W. Bush should be held responsible for intentionally lying to the American people. There was not a single authentic intelligence report to reflect that Saddam Hussein possessed WMD or that Iraq was connected to al-Qaeda or was a threat to the security of the U.S. As a matter of fact, Bin Laden viewed Saddam Hussein as a major threat for his and other Islamic militant groups whose intention is to replace secular regimes in the Arab world with Islamic ones.

The March 2006 New York Times article "Enemy of our Enemy" explains that prior to the Gulf War of 1990, Bin Laden warned that Iraq had designs on Persian Gulf states. The article states, "He even offered his own fighters to the Saudis in that war, making it clear that he yearned for the "infidel" dictator to be overthrown."

Under Saddam Hussein, the Iraqi government was the most secular regime in the Middle East. Despite its authoritarian nature, Hussein's regime included secular Shiaa, Christians and other minorities in high governmental positions. His regime was against

sectarianism and no attacks occurred on churches in Iraq until he was removed from power. Since then, sectarianism began to appear in Iraq and attacks against churches and some Sunni mosques began to take place. On December 25, 2013, BBC reported that a terrorist attack against Saint John Church in Baghdad caused the deaths of 28 people and injured 70 others.

This, of course, was not the first attack, nor will it be the last one, to take place in Iraq. Sectarian terrorism in Iraq due to the absence of security is also leading to civil war. Bush's war against Iraq led to the fulfillment of bin Laden's dream. Al-Qaeda and other Islamic terrorist groups are all over Iraq. Since the departure of American troops from Iraq at the end of 2011, more than 10,000 Iraqis have been killed by terrorism. The American public should remember that Bush's conquest of Iraq opened the doors to terrorism, not to democracy, as he claimed.

The present Iraqi government, under Prime Minister Nour al-Maliki, has turned into an authoritarian dictatorship with a clear policy of sectarianism. Even members of Iraq's parliament (especially the Sunni ones) have no immunity from prosecution or even death at the hands of al-Maliki's government. This policy opened up Iraq to al-Qaeda and other Islamic terrorist organizations. This is also

---

[34] David Corn, The Lies of George W. Bush: Mastering the Politics of Deception, Crown Publisher, 2003

(pp. 309)

reflected in the policy of al-Qaeda, who are involved in the civil war of neighboring Syria. They have already announced the establishment of the DAISH, which means the Islamic Emirate of Iraq and Syria. Again, bin Laden's philosophy is being implemented at least in theory. Again, this turn of political events reflects on the misguided American foreign policy.

Vincent Bugliosi, presented a strong case for the prosecution of George W. Bush for war crimes in Iraq.[35] He noted that, "George W. Bush could be put on trial in an American courtroom for the murder of nearly 4,500 American soldiers fighting the war in Iraq. Bush's invasion of Iraq was a war of choice. He and his vice president and their top aides and advisors should be held accountable for the lies and the fabrications of false intelligent reports, which they used to mislead the American population in order to justify the Iraqi invasion. President George W. Bush abused his executive privileges, and should be held accountable for his actions."

---

[35] Vincent Bugliosi, The Prosecution of George W. Bush for Murder, Vanguard Press, 2008

Citations

Bugliosi, Vincent. The Prosecution of George W. Bush for Murder. New York: Vanguard P, 2008.

Clarke, Richard A. Against all enemies inside America's war on terror. New York: Free P, 2004.

Corn, David. Lies of George W. Bush mastering the politics of deception. New York: Crown, 2003.

Greenspan, Alan. The Age of Turbulence Adventures in a New World. New York: Penguin P HC, The, 2007.

Mcclellan, Scott. What Happened. New York: PublicAffairs, 2008.

Suskind, Ron. The One Percent Doctrine Deep Inside America's Pursuit of Its Enemies Since 9/11. New York: Simon & Schuster, 2006.

Gelow, Amos and Labeed, Ifraeem. "Sixty Years of Israeli Secret Service: A Look From the Inside." Israeli Secret Service. 2010.

Kagan, Robert. "The World America Made." Vintage Press, 2012

Lebovich, Mark. "This Town." Penguin Group. 2013.

THE WORLD FACTBOOK (www.cia.gov) is the source of the map of Iraq on the cover page.

About the Author

Dr. Hani Fakhouri is a Professor Emeritus of Sociology and Anthropology at the University of Michigan Flint, where he taught from 1972 to 2000. He was department chair from 1979 to 1989.

He has written several books on cultural changes and transitions faced by Arabs, including *Kafr el Elow: Continuity and Change in an Egyptian Community, Kafr el Elow an Egyptian Village in Transition*, and a monograph entitled *Ethnicity and aging: Arab-American Elderly in Flint Michigan*.

He has had numerous articles published in scholarly journals such as the Oxford University Press and the Journal of the American Research Center in Egypt.

His blog, Middle East Today, focuses on current issues faced by Arabs within and without the region and can be accessed at http://www.mid-east-today.blogspot.com

www.ingramcontent.com/pod-product-compliance
Lightning Source LLC
Chambersburg PA
CBHW050817290526
45792CB00001B/153